# The Calling Of Joy!

# Books by Bruce Davis

The Magical Child Within You
The Heart of Healing
Monastery Without Walls
My Little Flowers
Simple Peace-the Spiritual life of St. Francis of Assisi

# The Calling Of Joy!

✦

## Unfolding Your Soul In Your Life

*Bruce Davis*

iUniverse, Inc.
New York  Lincoln  Shanghai

# The Calling Of Joy!
## Unfolding Your Soul In Your Life

Copyright © 2006 by Bruce L. Davis

iUniverse books may be ordered through booksellers or by contacting:

iUniverse
2021 Pine Lake Road, Suite 100
Lincoln, NE 68512
www.iuniverse.com
1-800-Authors (1-800-288-4677)


ISBN-13: 978-0-595-38868-4 (pbk)
ISBN-13: 978-0-595-83247-7 (ebk)
ISBN-10: 0-595-38868-X (pbk)
ISBN-10: 0-595-83247-4 (ebk)

Printed in the United States of America

# Contents

## *Appendix: Practical Spirituality*

# *Introduction*

Thirty years ago, I wrote a book titled, The Magical Child Within You. I was twenty something at the time. As I emerged into the adult world from college, I found an overwhelming sense of seriousness and great lack of joy. In the course of my studies in psychology, I learned there were many new therapies about remembering, reliving and remaking our childhood. However, there was little said about rediscovering and enjoying the inner child, the magical child within each of us. Today, of course the world offers the same seriousness and lack of joy. Cultivating innocence and peace, a life of great heart is as challenging now as ever.

In the demands of daily life, joy easily becomes a distant light. Yet when we feel the lightness of our joy, the same daily demands seem not so demanding. How do we live our joy in the midst of our troubled world? Why are some people who live with obvious difficulties like illness or lack of work still joyful while others who seemingly have everything, have everything but their joy? How does joy continue to find a home in some people while so many others lose their joyful nature? These questions have stayed with me as I explored other cultures and encountered many people with dancing hearts and brilliant eyes.

After nearly thirty years, the magical child has grown up. Well, if not grown up, he has at least aged. The calling of joy has resulted in a wonder full adventure. I find myself living in another country both literally and within myself. I am married to a partner who says with her entire being, "life is precious and meant for joy." I have adult children who just being themselves, are joy. My inner world could settle for nothing short of exploring life fully, discovering in the process that we really are a soul and have a life in eternity. Meanwhile life's events were not always easy. The path of joy was not a way around pain and challenges. Joy is a river, that when trusted, brings us through the pain and difficult events around us. At times, joy is an ocean that carries us through all that life presents. Joy is simple truth. This truth guides the choices we make moment to moment. The pure being we find inside, in each other and the world, is joy's body. With commitment to our hearts, we find no one is separate; no part of our selves is excluded. Joy is the peace found in this moment again and again. How do we open to this peace?

There is a voice inside each of us that says. "I am yearning for something more. I have a hunger that, no matter what I do or how much I have does not go away. This longing is never really silenced no matter how busy or comfortable I become. I can give up, compromise, and suppress this special part of myself. I can ignore my questions about who I am, what gives life meaning and what happens after this life. But sooner or later, I must know.

> The longing, the questions do not cease. I want to come home, home to my true self. And coming home is nothing less then coming inside to joy, my joy, to me."

Joy is much more then feeling good. Joy is more then happiness. Joy is a state of being. Joy is to live fully in the present moment. Joy is honesty. It is the courage to live my passion. Joy is creativity, tears, and laughter. Joy is my guide through life's many choices. It is the part of me I can always trust. I can feel joy in my body. I know it. Joy is truth. Joy is the vast space I find when I close my eyes and look inside. It is the freedom without limit I feel. Joy is who I am.

Life passes quickly and before we know it, the days become months and years with little or no joy. Only when we are opening to life's joy, are we really living. Life's purpose is to prepare us for the true joy, which is beyond, after this life. The tools to realize life's full journey, our true potential, are available. They are the tools the mystics have used through the ages. Modern psychology and spiritual pilgrims are rediscovering them again today. Joy's calling is perhaps the most important calling in our lives with nothing else its equal. There are a thousand excuses to live something other then our joy. And there is only one reason to live our joy. Joy is our essence. To hear the calling of joy is to hear the calling of our soul!

# I. A NEW BEGINNING

# Begin With the Small Things

Daily life for most everyone is difficult to manage. It is easy to lose track of our feelings, our dreams, and our selves. Every morning can be seemingly automatic. We wake up and begin thinking again about life's problems. One problem appears built on top of another and then another. Soon our joy is buried somewhere underneath. Diving into the pile of problems day after day, our hands seem to easily find more problems to grab onto while our joy remains out of reach.

How do we get to the bottom of the pile and find our joy again? Do we have to start at the top, solving one problem after another? Or is there another way? If joy is independent of having challenges in life, simply diving into the pile day after day is not the answer. Joy calls us to begin our day, even if only briefly, with the small things. How we begin each day says a lot how the day will proceed. If we begin in a hurry, busy, and anxious about everything that must be done, from the day's start, joy's small but important voice is suppressed. However, if we begin a little earlier and perhaps wake up slowly, listening to the sounds of nature or soft music, joy has a place in our life to grow.

> In the morning before we become busy with the details of life, another part of us is present. Our awareness is still soft and open from waking. In these moments our simple being is very close. There is an intimacy. An intimacy with all life is here to embrace us.

To begin the day with this embrace is a gift. In this space between waking and being fully involved in the issues of the day are many gifts. Life's presence inside us and around us is very present. Maybe joy begins by sitting quietly and enjoying the perfect cup of coffee. When the coffee is gone, joy calls us to sit enjoying the simple presence of life inside and out. Maybe joy is a walk in the garden to see what is blooming today before going to meetings or doing errands. Beginning the day with the small things reminds us of joy's importance and calling. Joy's voice is the perfect instrument to keep us in tune with our inner life, our feelings and intuition. While most people are busy from waking to going to sleep with what they believe are the big issues in life, joy calls us to the little flowers of life. The big issues will find their course in time but meanwhile there is life itself. Life's simple joys call again and again to be received and celebrated. Beginning the day with the small things is to reach into the inner world where the little moments give without ceasing. Beginning with the small moments each day, we have the opportunity to bring our awareness, our hearts, to what is present and receive deeply. This is to begin each day with an embrace. This is joy's domain.

# *Finding Real Food*

Joy calls us to search for and enjoy real food. More then our body needs nourishment, our hearts and souls hunger to be touched, to be fed. Where is there food for our soul in our lives? Often we are so busy with the details of life that we nearly forget about enjoying life itself. Life is more then daily survival. The daily schedule can quickly have time for everything and everyone else but no time for our self. It can become routine to be preoccupied with the chores of life with hardly a moment to enjoy life. Life is more than collecting comforts, more than battling stress. Joy calls. Everyday must have some time for real food. The day is not complete unless it includes food that feeds us deeply, food that nourishes the soul. Our thoughts are separated from our feelings and our feelings are separated from our soul, our essence. Real food, joy, heals this separation. Real food helps us feel our hearts, our core being once again. From our hearts, our feelings and thoughts, relationships and activities become connected again. We feel as one person, whole, and true.

Real food is life! Where do we feel most alive? With whom do we feel fully embraced? What are we doing when life is at its best? When are we really enjoying life? Real food is found in a safe place in our lives where we can let go of our struggles and enjoy the heart and beauty of the moment. Yes, real food is found in a safe place where we can relax, let go of everything we are carrying inside, and enjoy life. This maybe a walk through an old neighborhood or singing out our heart to the entire universe. Enjoying real food maybe sitting with last night's dream, feeling again and again what opens inside of us. Real food may be standing a minute or two longer with a stranger in the street or canceling everything and spending a whole day with our children. Real food can be listening to our inner child and having fun. Communion in Church or taking the time to simply sit quietly in one's own heart, are all sources of real food. Real food, joy, is the embrace of life, God, the cosmic intimacy. Each day is incomplete without joy.

There is no motivation for joy other than joy itself. We do not seek real food because it will improve our careers, further our education, find new friends, or necessarily find solutions to our difficulties. We seek real food because it is true. Some find real food practicing yoga or Tai Chi. They practice not only for physical fitness. They practice for the simple joys of being alive in their body. Others find real food sitting with a Holy Book or picture. They feel the presence from the words or picture in their hearts and all around them. Their joy is to sit on the lap of God. Real food in any form is this love, this intimacy. Real food can be dancing until two in the morning. Then instead of joining friends for drinking and small talk, real food may be going outside and standing under the stars in the silence. As the others go home tired with a feeling of alcohol, it is joy to go home with the stars still dancing inside of us. The path of real food is not always what is easiest or what is comfortable. It is listening to another voice inside of us. Our souls are yearning, calling out.

Real food can be making a journal of life's golden moments. People easily remember past negative experiences. Recalling memories of deepest joy, writing them down in exquisite detail, reading and rereading them again is to remember the moments of our soul alive in the world. In modern culture we think we need a new experience again and again to feel alive. In other cultures, people often remember great stories, past dreams, miraculous events to remind them of God's presence and the power of creation in their lives. We can remember our personal moments of pure joy as the path of affirming real food in the life of our soul. Memories recalled are no longer in the past but is food now once again feeding our hearts and well of being.

Real food can be going to the parts of town no-one goes to and giving food to the people who are living there, homeless. Their expressions of gratitude are worth a hundred times more then our time spent preparing the food for them. Real food may be telephoning an old friend we have not spoken with because of a misunderstanding. Instead of avoiding each other, one short call may be real food for both of us. Many people are active in gardening, art, and music. But do we take the time to enjoy and receive the beauty in the midst of our activity?

*Beauty in any form is God's presence in our lives, feeding our soul.*

In many cultures there is a holiday of giving thanks. Real food is in all the love preparing the meal, the joining of family and friends, in the abundant feeling of love that is present. The anticipation, the event, and memories are all part of the nurturing. Gratitude can virtually turn any experience into real food by the opening of the heart.

### *Slowing Down*

What almost all experiences of real food have in common is the experience of slowing down. We are often in a hurry to get somewhere or are generally just in a hurry. We can be in a hurry by habit. We rarely take the time to just be, to be soft, and open to this moment. No matter what form, real food becomes more substantial the more present we are. In this moment we remember joy's abundance. Often we do not take the time for anything that does not have practical value, for anything outside of business or family. There is no time for personal longings. But what is time for? What gives life meaning if there is no time for us, our hearts, for joy?

*Slowing down frees us from the busy, fearful energy of the daily world to a fresh awareness. The moment we begin a life of real food, our lives begin a new course. Real food demands we slow down and receive the moment. Life's essence cannot be hurried. The moment we slow down, our awareness begins to find something more. It spreads to a larger horizon then our normal thoughts. Our awareness lands softly in the moment.*

What is here? This moment often escapes us because we are coming from or going to, planning, or reacting to events around us.

When we are with real food, we are landing in a new moment. No matter where we are, no matter the circumstances around us, there is something fresh and present that feeds us. It may be the birds singing, the colors in the clouds, the gentle eyes of a friend, the soft hand of our partner. Taking the time to receive this moment reminds us, embraces us, renews us in a special way.

We seek real food because our souls call us. When the soul is fed, mind and body are well. When our soul is not fed, our whole being suffers. Nothing less then joy feeds the longing, the hunger that is deeper than material things. Joy is the pure food that speaks to the pure place inside of us. Without joy, life is complicated, confused, compromised. Our days are busy with obligations, chores, surviving. Life's pure presence, the simple beauty, is lost. With joy, we find renewed clarity. We find renewal. Our health, family, work, activities prosper. But if we tell others that we are living for joy, usually we receive little support. Joy is something selfish, a waste of time. Joy is something better not to speak about but to a select few. And even he or she may not be very supportive. There certainly must be others things more important for us to do? If you say, "I spend time sitting at sunrise" or "I often take a walk under the stars before going to sleep, listening to the silence," most people would understand but nevertheless not take the time themselves for such pursuits. Those around us usually are thinking, "What is important is what we are doing. It's nice you have time for such trivial things. I am much too busy. It sounds too selfish." And this is the problem. We are all much too busy. Life is selfish or in other words full of self. But what are we doing with ourselves? What do we have to give when we are full of stress or constantly running around feeling empty inside? Perhaps real selfishness is not receiving the gifts of life and sharing these gifts with the world. Perhaps true selfishness is our lack of joy and gratitude for all that is given.

Meanwhile, real food, joy, calls into question, "What is our busy-ness all about? What are we doing with our lives?" Real food is to take a step out of the busy-ness of our daily life and into the sanctuary of our heart. A life with no room for the soul is destined for the myriad of problems of separation. We are separated from each other, nature, our purpose, our selves, our soul. A life with no space for the soul is without meaning just a road of unconnected events. The calling of joy is to make time and space. Joy is the food that gives us awareness that we are a soul. Slowly this awareness grows. Our soul unfolds in our lives.

## *Making Choices*

Joy is not something we can catch one day, hold onto, and have ready whenever we want. Real food is something special. There are no guarantees. Joy comes from risking, opening and receiving. It is a little like swimming. We can think about swimming. We can read books and discuss swimming. We can walk around the pool and imagine swimming. But only when we go swimming do we begin to know the experience. Joy is getting wet, really wet. There is a big difference between thinking about joy and living joy.

Real food teaches us it is as important to create life's precious moments, as it is to surrender to each moment. Each day is full of choices. What is our awareness pursuing? Fulfilling work is found in the many moments when our hearts are present. Similarly, true relationships are found in the many moments we are present and available to one another. Are we occupied with only life's struggle? How do we think the struggle will end unless we make a new course? The compromises continue until we find food that feeds our being. Most people are waiting for some big event, vacation, retirement, or new position in life. Others simply give up hope. Each moment of joy is what is important. Each moment full of joy strengthens our heart, our trust, our knowing.

With real food our thoughts touch down in God's vast garden. Joy is creating and surrendering, reaching out to what is important and letting go of what is not important. This is a daily practice. Beholding what is important and letting go of what is not important. This commitment leads to the perfect food. Joy in any form is joy. Are we listening or have we turned off our passion? If there is no real food in our life, it is better to be honest with our self, rather than just living. It is better to be aware, that we are living in a desert. The search for real food will point our heart again in the right direction. Something substantial, something true will come. The next step always comes! The answer lies not in the big things in life, making new plans for careers, partnerships, or family. The answer lies in the moment. The big decisions will come naturally when we have real food, turning the moment into something precious and sacred.

For those who feel separate from their river, themselves, joy may begin by knowing what is not joy! By choosing less what we do not enjoy, we slowly make the effort to be more with ourselves again, life's river. We become available for what gives us joy. As we begin to make choices between joy and compromises we normally live with, we are practicing honesty with ourselves. We are following less the excuses we have that keep us from joy. The path of letting go of our fears and choosing joy may begin by looking at our calendar. We begin making more appointments with joy and fewer compromises from fear. We practice living from our river, our passion, and our truth.

Each day, our inner hunger speaks to us. Maybe we will run in the forest nearby. Maybe we will sit a half hour and feel everything in our heart. Running or sitting, we can slowly let our worries and concerns go and feel the soft presence of life. We can feel our wild breath, free. We can feel ourselves. Real food is an impulse to rediscovering our souls. This impulse may come from an enlightening book or teaching, a sacred church or flower garden nearby. Each joy is an impulse to open to our essence. In these moments and the moments afterwards, we feel as if our soul is breathing. We feel alive.

Real food is embracing our inner being. The experience of what we call God, our eternal self, or pure being begins in feeling our own presence. Taking the time to feel our own presence apart from the demands and noise of the world is the beginning of the exploration of life's greatest calling inside of us. Slowly, we experience our simple presence deepening and expanding. There is something more. There is a greater presence. Apart from the daily world, our awareness rests and spreads in a vast space.

> *God is not separate from us. Real food brings our attention to something more, life's perfect presence expanding inside of us and in the world.*

We take a fresh look at what is important in our calendar. Where is there real food? Making a schedule involves listening as well as choosing. Real food is in not making plans as well as the planning. It is not how much time is set aside for real food but that time exists for real food. With real food, life becomes inspired. Real food is passion. What gives us passion? While others are busy with desires of having something more and something bigger, we are yearning and reaching for the presence of life itself. We have a passion for life! The path is joy. Real food awakens our sleeping soul.

Having a path of nourishing our hearts keeps us in the river of our abundant being. Here our awareness expands to new horizons and new depths of life's simple and rich presence. Here we discover the relationships, work, activities, which are natural for us, which are who we are. Real food is returning us to a passionate inner life to once again find treasure in the world. Real food is also reminding us of a place greater than anything in this world. This place is overlooked and forgotten. Our soul is worlds of being, beyond words, waiting inside of us to be received.

# *Desires, No Desires, Beyond Desires*

When we have real food in our lives we do not have so many desires. When we take the time to feed ourselves deeply each day, we do not need so many things and activities to keep us busy. Most people desire something bigger and more because inside they feel little and less. They need a large house, new car, or lots of expensive clothing because they are living separate from their joy everyday. When we are enjoying life, we are living in our stream of great being. Having expensive possessions, importance in the eyes of others, and special vacations are not so important. Life is a vacation. Life is joy.

People need lots of things when they have no-thing happening inside of them. They need to impress others when they feel little inside for themselves. No amount of success in the world can overcome a life that does not feel successful. Accumulating friends does not heal a heart that is lonely and separate from joy. No amount of possessions can make a difference for someone who feels unworthy and does not possess their own passion and vital being. A vacation spent lying in the sun worrying about life's problems and struggling with our selves is not really a vacation. The struggles continue until joy feeds and heals the hurts we carry. Until then, the hurts follow us wherever we go. The desire for more and more continues until we live in joy's river. Joy, our vast being, is the "more" and the "bigger" that we really desire.

No matter how much we shop and consume, life is still empty when we do not have ourselves. Success and importance in the world are no replacement for feeling successful and important. These feelings come from living and nurturing our true being. People, who feel powerless, need more and more power. Those who feel of little value need lots of praise from others. No amount of comfort can help someone who is not comfortable with themselves. Endless activity will not satisfy someone who is afraid to be alone with nothing to do. Companionship naturally comes for someone who finds beauty in his or her own company. There will always be something wrong with our friends or partner until we find and enjoy what is right in ourselves. Life, no matter how we try to make it, is missing something when we are missing our joy. And when we are missing our joy, our soul, our greater being remains far away.

Our father can be ill. Our job may be ending. Our best friend may be busy and unavailable. Our child may be failing in school. And we can still have joy.

> *Joy is something inside of us that the world ultimately cannot give or take away from us. When we have our joy, we become clearer with all of our desires.*

Fulfilling ourselves physically and emotionally can be real food as love and peace are absorbed deeper into our being. And physical and emotional desires can be less important as something deeper inside of us is being fed and listened to. A life of joy leads us to find the difference between fulfilling desires that momentarily satisfy some insecurity and the desires, which come from deep within us. We value what is important and let go of the wishes that are not so important. With joy we are less judgmental and critical. Joy builds our self-esteem leading us to more choices of joy.

Often we have lots of desires because our desire for simple peace and well being seems so far out of reach. We pursue having more and more because we do not know how to enjoy what we have. There is never enough for anyone who has not found that they are enough. The voice inside, "I want. I want", rules our thoughts until we find the awareness that says, "I am." Until we rediscover and live our essence, we are not satisfied. There are always problems as long as we live separate from ourselves. We can study more, make career changes, seek new friends but nothing we do in the world makes a difference as long as we are living separate from our simple being, our passion, our truth. Many of our desires are merely bold attempts to grasp something that we must find inside ourselves. And when we have ourselves, our desires are much more simple, immediate, and direct. Life is simple, immediate, and direct. Joy is never very far away when we are close to ourselves. Real food is here when we are ready to receive and to give.

## *Desires Can Show Us the Way*

There are desires, which are part of our life force, our joy. And there are desires, which keep us busy and take us away from our heart's true wishes. There are desires, which express our creativity, our joy. And there are desires that let off steam and keep us merely comfortable. There is a world of little desires which keep our days occupied. And there are life's grand desires, our longing, our quests.

Desires big or small are only desires. They are not so important either to fulfill or ignore. People spend so much energy fighting some desires and struggling for others. How can we say "yes" to some parts of ourselves and "no" to other parts and think we can end up with peace? Life is not a competition of desires. Life is an opportunity to feel our deepest desire. When we take the time to feel our longing, our true thirst and hunger, the little desires control less and less of our awareness during the day. Our true desire can call forth the teacher, lover, work, the joy that will really serve us. Our true desire is our friend, guiding us to more life, meaning, and joy. Our deepest desire calls for full life, God, to come home again inside. To listen to our deepest longing is to hear the calling of our soul. We want to be patient and understanding with the cries of our soul.

Desires are not something to punish ourselves for. Desires are not something to struggle for and find disappointment. Desires tell us something about our separation from our river of joy. As we commit ourselves to our greatest joys, our desires become less and our simple joyful being becomes more.

> *Desires are not meant to rule our life but gently guide us back into our own river, our being, where desires are already satisfied.*

There is truth in each of our desires when we take the time to be with them, listen and receive them. So often we quickly try to satisfy our desires or stop them as if they should not exist. But they do exist. Desires are not our enemy to quickly silence one way or another. Our desires tell us something about our hearts, our inner stream. Opening to our desires, listening, being, receiving them maybe more important then finding a solution. Our desires express our life energy, our life force. Our desires when held gently can take us to our source of joy, our source of being. How we live our desires says much about how we embrace or reject life and the many gifts presented to us everyday.

Many people ask if the path is to be full of self, having a life full of worldly and personal joys? Or are we to become self less, free of desires, free of worldly and personal needs? If we listen to joy's calling, are we becoming full of self or called to become free by being selfless? Is the true life to have our desires for family, income, and success? Or is joy's path beyond having our desires fulfilled and becoming desire less, in fact selfless? What is the way to true freedom? The answer is to be true to ourselves.

## *Recovering Our Deeper Longing*

There are seasons for the different parts of life. There is a season for education and careers. There is a season to be parents. There is a season for purely personal exploration. There is a season to fulfill many places in the heart. When we are not busy making some desires wrong and others right, we can more clearly hear our own season. Life naturally has stages to fulfill different parts of ourselves. We are at peace and clear with each stage in life as we are true to our self, our river of joy. Often we have an inner competition of desires going on. We want to have partnership and we want to be alone. We want lots of income and we want to live simply. This inner competition results in having two rivers running. Desires are fighting one another for control. Which do we choose?

Joy's path is bringing these rivers back together. The inner steps of heartfulness, understanding, help us be true to our season. By loving our small self, it does not have so many needs separate from our deeper longing. The path is neither embracing all our desires nor giving up our desires. There is no intellectual decision or discipline in one direction or the other that heals a divided heart. Our separation is healed one moment at a time. The question is, where we are in this moment? The answer is in the joy our awareness is discovering. The answer is in living with real food that is nourishing us deeply, healing our divisions between mind and heart, the separation in our heart from our soul.

Having our desires fulfilled or giving up our desires is not as important as knowing what are our true desires. Which desires are coming from our fears of wanting security, status, or self-importance? And which of our desires are coming from our passion for life? To fulfill our desires, which come from fear, only result in more desire. We never have enough possessions, power, and importance when fear is at the root of these desires. We never find ourselves really secure. We want more and more. Our fears are in the driver's seat of our daily choices. With fear in control, our desires fulfilled or not, bring us little joy. Real food heals the fear stirring up desires by touching fear's roots, embracing us until we are free.

Meanwhile, when we let go of our desires that come from our true passion, we take away part of our truth, our heart. Our true passions are a guide for us to listen to and follow. Often people accept the desires they think they should and reject the others. They are dividing themselves, separating from their life force. Our true passion comes from our river of life. Our passions are our creativity, our beauty, community, and service. They are our joys, small and large which we are bringing into the world. To cut off these desires is to cut back the gifts we have for the world. Fulfilling our desires or letting go of our desires is understood as we nourish ourselves with real food. Instead of dreaming of our desires and living a life of compromise, joy's presence fulfills and guides us each day. Our true passion is full of life energy. At times this passion can be our sexuality. At other times this passion is for peace, the peace without words, the peace beyond words, the peace inside of peace. The questions to be self-full or self less fall away every time we go inside, receive, and be the great peace we find.

As we grow closer to our essence, our passion changes. As we grow closer to our essence our sense of self becomes clearer. The path of joy brings us closer day by day to our essence. Out of our essence, our self emerges. Some days this self may be full of worldly desires. Other days this self simply is, no desire, only joy. Nourishing and remembering our essence, the separate selves, endless desires slowly come home.

## Being True to Ourselves

Some people think they should let go of having lots of possessions and desires. They should lead a life of no possessions, no desires. So they make a radical change in their lives. But inside, their struggles continue. Some people can be as concerned and attached to one simple set of clothing as others are concerned about maintaining their big house. Leaving our normal freedom to live, sleep, eat, and vacation as we wish for strict beliefs telling us what we can do, when to sleep, and what we can eat, may seem dramatic and full of promise. But will these beliefs result in making us free inside? The heart and soul cannot be organized for joy. Joy's path is listening, trusting, and being true to ourselves.

When we are told to give up something, we feel rebellious. We feel deprived. When we find a greater joy and then give up something, it is easy, natural. When we give up something because we are told to do it, some part of us feels resentful. Often our attachment and struggle shifts from one thing to another, one behavior to another, from our old identity to a new one. It may look like we are living differently but usually we are only wearing different clothes. We are living with new beliefs, maybe eating different foods. Inside we are more or less the same.

> *The changes we make in our outer life have little consequence for our inner awareness if they are not the fruit of true joy. Real change comes from real food that is nourishing our lives. Real change comes from the inside outwards into our lives.*

When we have a daily practice of real food, we literally cannot digest false foods, things that really do not nourish us. Our feelings know what is true for us. We cannot live a life that does not honor who we are. When we find real joy, we are not interested in chasing after possessions, desires, small and large, that really do not feed us. When we have real food we are not in conflict with our desires. Our desires are beautiful, expressions of our heart. Real food brings us to the seat of joy, our soul.

# *Finding our Security*

We contract from life, reject our desires because we are often more concerned with our security. The opposite of joy is fear. Concerns for security keep fears, large and small, nearby and grabbing for our awareness. There is always something to pull the heart away from joy. Normally, we think our security is in our work, family, and activities in the world. Life in the world, however, is always changing. There is no secure job. Relationships change. Life is change, and with change, fear is always near by. The truth is, as long as we live our lives separate from real food, our joy, fear is nearby. With fear comes insecurity. As long as we live separate from real food, we are just passing time. We are lonely and without joy. Fears, large and small, rule our day.

In modern times it is normal to project our thoughts and feelings, our desires and well being out into the world. We see the daily world as our source of security and fulfillment. What is important is what we are doing and how much we have. What we have in the bank is more important then what we carry in our hearts. Our simple being, our well of peace inside is unsupported and left unexplored. In our search outside ourselves for the answers, success, and comfort we seek, we separate ourselves from our river of joy. We often believe in others before trusting ourselves. We are constantly reaching outside to find relief for our anxieties. Our awareness does not know how to rest inside, to celebrate our passion, and be secure in our own gentle heart.

### *How Children Are Losing Their Inner Security*

This search outside ourselves begins when we are quite small. The separation from trusting ourselves, enjoying and resting in our inner being begins at an early age. Beginning as infants we are pushed to "grow up", to do more, to learn more, to accomplish more and more. Children quickly learn to conform to the emotional needs and schedules of the parents. They understand they must adjust to the demands of the world if they are to get the love they want. Beginning at an early age, parents pass on their own fears and needs about being successful. The unique parent, who is secure in their own being, naturally trusts the child in their own development. The child is given the gift to mature in his or her own way and time.

We have lost our balance between honoring and listening to the inner life and meeting the expectations of our competitive society. Early in life, making the child wrong for their feelings and desires starts the blocking of the inner stream of joy. Early in life, children begin hearing "no" more then "yes". Natural passions are blocked or guided into more "productive" activities. Children's joy for example, in playing, daydreaming, or singing to themselves, are channeled towards more "practical" interests. Beginning at an early age, passions are often thwarted for something parents and teachers consider of more value. Soon, passion is no longer felt as children learn to behave as others think they should. Trust in themselves and others are lost. They begin feeling disconnected, separate and restless. Children in the modern world are losing their joy.

Children need support to be themselves, to listen and feel as much as to speak and do something. Daily life needs room to express personal choices and not just follow what is the program. Choices are the source of their creativity. Through having choices, the heart feels embraced and expresses its uniqueness.

The soul of each child calls to take time to feel their feelings, find words for their experience, to open life's gifts slowly, naturally. Instead of always having toys ready, the next planned activity; children need to be allowed to simply be. Always entertaining children prepares them for a life that always needs entertainment. People do not know how to enjoy their own company. Life is a toy. Joy is everywhere. There is no competition between the inner and the outer world.

> *It is not a question of learning to read or learning to listen to our feelings and intuition. A happy child is innocent and true in their being. They are always learning. A full inner life gives us passion, love, trust for making a life that is true and productive in the world.*

What parents fail to realize is that play, daydreaming, singing to ourselves, is the expression of our inner life. When these expressions are made wrong, our life force glows dimmer, withdraws. When our passions are supported, our inner fire thrives. We feel our joy in all our body, our being. Our passions may or may not someday earn us income, but our joy gives us something more then income. It gives us security. It gives us our wholeness, our well being. Passion expresses our truth. Living our passion is unfolding our soul in our lives.

Parents and teachers who do not trust themselves, their own paths of joy, are not likely to trust the passion and natural development of their children. Instead, parents feel more secure when their child is successful. Success is how soon children crawl, talk, act and do what they should be doing at a particular age. Parents and teachers are especially proud when their children know the alphabet and do basic math at age three. No one is noticing the expression of their hearts, the excitement of their joy. The result is that most adults are more successful at math than personal relationships. We are more productive working for others than making a life for ourselves. We know more about science than our own feelings.

When children are forced to learn before they are hungry to learn, the information is stored on top of feelings, which are pushed aside. The demands of the school system are pushing the children's natural essence, their innocence into the background. Intelligence, which is not connected to feeling, which is not connected to our essence, is a life separate from our soul. Knowledge is developed at the expense of trusting our feelings, honoring our passions, our creativity and joy. Intelligence is developed at the expense of unfolding our souls. We have lots of information on all kinds of subjects but know little about our own awareness, our feelings, and our desires, our inner being. Awareness of our inner beauty disappears. The development of the inner arts of surrender, creativity, humility, service, inner peace have to be found in some other part of life, if found at all. Our inner resources have been sacrificed for knowledge about everything else. Educators forget what makes us successful is to first know ourselves.

Parents and teachers of young children could be reminded that our greatest natural resource, our children, need our shelter, love, and protection. Complicated demands, early verbal skills, and expectations for success are robbing them of their greatest asset, the joy of innocence. Parents and teachers of older children could be teaching universal human values like peace, nonviolence, truth, and right action. These values give the soul important structure for expression in the world. And parents and teachers of young adults could be offering the steps to inner development including heartfulness, understanding, compassion, forgiveness, and wisdom. The inner life of young people does not have to be abandoned for intellectual progress and achievement. Our inner life is the ground upon which successful achievement in the world is built. Children who are acknowledged for their feelings including what gives them joy become adults clear on their feelings and the life of joy that calls them.

> *Children, who are supported in their inner life, naturally find their talent. Their talent will grow and guide them in the world. Each child's talent, is their path of joy into adulthood.*

Intelligence does not have to be at the expense of a life of joy. When personal development excludes our inner life, people end up having a house in the world with little or no foundation. They have a career, relationships, and many activities but their inner being, trust, capacity of heart and joys are limited. A successful outer world unconnected to a passionate inner life is empty, separate, and lonely. No matter how successful people may become, their lack of inner development handicaps them in life. Their joy is fleeting and seemingly always apart from them. They are not connecting with their source. They do not feel their peace, their inner fire.

As parents we naturally have limited capacity to love our children, to give and be present as much as we would like. We are busy and our children quickly begin mirroring this life of hyper activity. There is always so much to do, that we cannot sit more then a few minutes, quietly, simply receiving our child. We cannot give our children, what we, ourselves are missing, inner peace and well being. So the cycle continues. Our children learned early that security is projected in how much they achieve and succeed. How good we are depends upon how successful we are in the world.

## *Finding Peace, Safety and Joy Inside of Us*

Eventually we learn there is no substitute for joy. No amount of money, no guarantee of comfort, no security in the world will give joy. Joy is something we have to open to and receive each day. There is no substitute for living our passion. Being connected to ourselves deeply is our true security.

> *With joy, work can change, relationships can change, and life can change. Joy is something independent. It is something in us, which cannot be taken away. It is who we are.*

As long as we think our security is outside of our self, fear is prevalent and joy limited. Some days there is much success and other days there is little. Sometimes we are with good friends and other times we are alone. But we have our own treasure. We have our selves, our vast inner landscape.

Many people think you either have security in the world or you go off into cave or monastery somewhere and find inner peace. They do not understand security is not a question of one or the other. Many people think they can have either a successful outer life or must have nothing and a reclusive inner life. We can have both. We need both. We need a developed inner life of feelings, hopes, dreams, intuition, depths of peaceful being. Then we can have a strong and effective outer life of relationships, work, and activity. However, in our culture we are out of balance. Real life is thought to be what we do in the world. We are invested in our outer security, our careers, and our investments. We have little understanding of how to build and enjoy our inner life, to have true security.

For some people, real security maybe learning how to be "lazy". In our compulsive world we are doing, doing constantly. Taking an afternoon free, a day, several days just for ourselves, may be the beginning to finding ourselves again, our passion, our truth, our well of being. There are always reasons to keep busy. But being lazy in the eyes of others, even our own eyes, may be an important beginning to find our real truth. Being lazy may be the beginning of appreciating life for itself and not being worried about what others are thinking and what we are producing. Stopping everything we are doing may be the beginning of finding our passion for life again, our reason for being. When we are living without passion, we are living separate, disconnected, and anxious. When the heart is full of worldly concerns there is no room to feel our selves, our peace. When our inner being is occupied with only worldly thoughts and problems we cannot come to our essence. Fear runs through our veins.

Some people are afraid to become available for joy. What will happen if I stop and begin feeling my feelings? Maybe it will all be too much. Maybe I will quit my job or leave my family. Maybe people will think I am strange. Maybe, maybe, maybe everything will change and I will never be the same. Much fear is present. The search and enjoyment of real food begins slowly, one experience, one moment, at a time. Slowly our fears lessen and our sense of self strengthens. There are no answers for the thousand questions that flood the mind. These questions come from our fear. Each joy received, calmly, heals and lessens our separation from our self.

Most people will never go through this process. They will never be free of their fears. They remain locked in a life waiting for something to change. Working, they wait for a vacation or pension. Family, they wait for someone else to be different. Before they know it, they find themselves locked in the limitations of old age. They remained trapped in a lifestyle where everyone is trying to be comfortable, while inside they are afraid and lonely. With little joy, they have too much fear to let go of their job and explore other possibilities. With little self-confidence, they have little strength to love more their family and to find a path that is true for everyone. Life passes by. Meanwhile, someone who knows their joy can have two or three careers in one lifetime. They can let go and begin again. They can have new relationships, new friends, new activities, new life, no matter how old they are or how much money they have. Without joy, we are frozen, unable to change. With joy there are unlimited possibilities.

# What Happens to Joy When There is Difficulty?

When pressure at work builds, when there is conflict or illness in the family, when life's difficulties come upon us, there is seemingly every feeling at these times other than joy. In these moments we are hurt and react with sadness, anger, or fear. We may bury our feelings somewhere inside and try to cope with more compromise. Living separate from our passion in life, we are separate from our fire, our strength, and inner peace. When we have few inner resources, life's stress is felt more intensely. When we have little room for joy in our lives in general, in difficult times the hope for joy is even less. However, if we are living daily our joy, we have much more capacity to be with life's challenges. Our hurt and anger is still present but not so overwhelming. We have more of ourselves, more of our heart energy in every situation. Our reactions to life's difficulties are more full of hope and possibilities. When we live our joy, difficulty is felt completely, but so is recovery. Joy is the great healer.

The life of joy is not a blind life, denying what is occurring around us. The violence in our world, both physical and emotional is real. Joy's calling is to build a life of inner resources, discovering and living in our well of being. We are called even more to joy when there is suffering. Then we have more of our entire being, God's presence with us and in us to be with the challenges. How someone responds to suffering who is living a life of frustration and compromise is very different than how we respond when we are daily living our joy and heart's true energy. This is why the daily life of having real food, a life that nourishes us is important. Life is more than living from one stressful event to the next. Joy's life invites us to be and give the most to the suffering in our midst.

Joy's calling includes the beauty and love in serving others. Often the people who are talking most about the problems of the world are the people who are doing the least about them. The people who are really feeding the poor, reaching out to the lonely, being with the dying, talk less and are giving the most. They know the true joy of serving. They know joy's passion; the heart's fire, as it burns away fear, moves obstacles, and brings joy to others. Joy's life naturally leads to service as our joy spreads and lifts the darkness within and around us.

With joy in our lives, we react differently to pain and life's challenges. We naturally are being and giving more. The life of joy builds strong muscles of the heart and soul. The strength of our heart and awareness of our soul sustain us. We have reserves to fall back upon. Our inner being has the strength that gives us power for faster and more complete recovery. A difficulty for one person may make them question everything in their life, their activities, their relationships, and their values. The same difficulty for someone, who is living his or her joy, is only a difficulty, nothing more. Everything in life is not questioned. The bumps in the road do not make us question the entire journey.

On joy's path, we see our difficulties differently. We see the compromises we make that increase our pain. Often our difficulties are just our normal complicated life but now only more complicated.

*Challenges at work, in relationships, even illness and loss rarely come suddenly without some warning. The signals were there if we were not too invested in keeping everything the same, too fearful of change. On joy's path we are more open to seeing what is true for us.*

We let others be themselves and express their needs. We have ourselves, so we let others have their desires and needs. Knowing our own weaknesses and feelings, we understand the feelings and limitations of the others. Being less caught in the web of our own pain; we can see the actions of others coming from their own pain and limitations. We do not punish ourselves for having difficulties. And we do not punish others for not fulfilling our expectations.

## We are the Ocean

Life is like an ocean. Normally we live on the surface with the waves of daily life splashing and sometimes crashing around us and over us. Perhaps we learn to swim with the waves or between them. We learn to survive. Maybe we build a small or large boat. We are busy taking care and managing our boat with the sea's daily winds. We try to stay comfortable. The life of joy calls our awareness to explore the ocean. There is an ocean of being inside of us. This is the next world for modern man to discover! Most people do not know to close their eyes and let their awareness go deep inside, into their hearts. The ocean is inside of us as well as outside. When we find this vast space inside we learn to rest. We can fully rest in our ocean. The ocean inside of us is our well of being. When we live only in the activity, the waves of daily life, we are busy doing something all the time with little time for being. As much as we live in the daily world, we can also live underneath the waves, in our ocean. The ocean supports us in the waves of daily life. Whether we have a small boat or large one, our awareness can include the ocean. The waves come and go. Sometimes they are crashing all around us. Sometimes everything is quiet, the water is still. As we explore and discover our joy, our inner resources, we find an ocean of awareness. This ocean carries us through life, its storms and peaceful beauty. This is very different then living only in the waves of today's activity and being tossed about.

Our soul calls us to a life in the great ocean. We are not here to be tossed about from one drama to another. We have more purpose then to spend life bouncing in the waves of difficulty. The life of joy gives us a much greater self to bring to our challenges. With our greater being, the challenges are often seen as something else. They are opportunities for loving more ourselves and others. They call us to find joy's presence even in the midst of hardship.

As we let go of our fears, joy brings us to the ocean of our being. All our feelings, our anger, our sadness, tears and laughter are a part of joy's being. Each feeling is joy because each feeling that is true is life itself. It feels good to cry, to laugh, and to feel our anger or sadness. It feels good to feel! This is joy, being able to feel. Joy is feeling our river of truth, of life. As we are true to ourselves, the river of our being grows wider, stronger, bringing us to our inner ocean, a vast awareness. We are breathing in God's ocean, only most people do not experience this. Their fears, their busy-ness keeps them separate. Their fears keep them struggling on the surface, grasping to hold on to something, to control the waves around them. Fear keeps them from experiencing and expressing their feelings.

Our fears keep us small. Joy makes us big. The life of fear includes relationships and work, which make us feel small. We all have had friends who are jealous or sceptical of our joys. And we have friends who support us to risk and experience as much life as possible. The path of joy is choosing friends, work, a life, which support us to feel big. Joy is the Great Ocean calling us. Our soul unfolds in our lives as we choose friends and activities that support our joy, to feel big and wonder full. The awareness of our soul is vast, too precious to be kept in a silent corner of our life and not shared and celebrated.

To find joy, we must take the time, open our hearts and experience. Joy should be no more difficult for adults then for children. Children naturally live in joy. Our difficulty finding joy is a statement of how far we have grown from ourselves, our inner child, our innocence, our essence.

# No to Self-Sacrifice, Suffering, and Guilt

Many of our difficulties are of our own making. We are accepting the beliefs of those around us and in modern culture that self-sacrifice is good, that suffering is normal, and we should feel guilty if we live differently from what others expect of us. It is common to feel supported in being miserable. We say to each other, "This is our cross to carry. This is bad karma or God's will. Suffering creates strength of character. A little pain is good for you. No one promises you a garden of roses. God loves the hurting, the poor, the hungry." Our culture is full of messages that it is normal, indeed good to be unhappy. No! God is love! Truth and joy create strength of character. Pain in any form is pain. How did love and suffering become so confused?

Life at times may include self-sacrifice, suffering, or feelings of guilt, but these are not reasons for living. We are not here to sacrifice ourselves. We are not here to suffer. We are not here to live in guilt from sin or judgement from someone else. We are alive. This is a gift. Life is a gift of joy. We are called to open to and receive life. Anything less than receiving fully the gifts we are given is to cut short our true purpose and potential. We do not need to be made to suffer or feel guilty to do the right thing. When our hearts are well and joyful, our conscience naturally tells us the right thing to do. Our conscience, God's voice inside of us, is most clear when not covered over with the dark clouds of self-sacrifice, suffering, and guilt.

We sacrifice ourselves, giving up upon on our hearts, in the name of family, tradition, social roles, career, religion, or merely out of habit. Our passion for life withers as we meet the demands and expectations of others. We suffer, as we find no other choice but to follow the prescribed path. We feel guilty when we begin considering another course, a course more for ourselves. Life can be sacrifice, suffering, and feelings of guilt because we find no other way.

Sometimes we need to find someone who needs us. Then we sacrifice ourselves for the needs of the other. We become slaves to work, projects, to life instead of being masters of finding our joy. Sacrifice and suffering can make us feel important and needed. We do not have to find what really makes us happy. We do not have to risk living our true passion and fire for life. We surrender our own wishes and dreams for others. People around us are impressed by how sacrificing we are.

### A Prison of Our Own Making

Suffering can be a way of life. We can easily fall into a pattern of giving up on ourselves, giving up on life. Often we can be working for everything but ourselves, our own development. Relationships can be two people joined in sacrifice. It becomes a circle without joy. Life as sacrifice, suffering, and feelings of guilt is ultimately empty, time consuming, fruitless. We can live behind walls of separateness, lonely, thinking this is normal life. Joy is something read about in magazines or happening to others in movies.

We all at times feel as if we are prisoners to the circumstances of our lives. We wait for someone or something to somehow come to the rescue and set us free. Few people talk about their prison as if it is of their own making. Instead they take comfort in their excuses. People take heart in hearing that compromise and disappointment are normal everywhere for just about everyone. People are admired and rewarded for self-sacrifice and suffering. Have you ever heard of anyone being rewarded and celebrated for finding and living their joy? Have you ever heard of someone being honored for their joyful heart, their joyful life? What lifts the world more then joy?

Meanwhile, most of us do not know the experience of true joy. After a lifetime of others saying "no" to us and saying "no" to ourselves, our hearts become dull and hard. We have been living for so long how others expect us to live, that we no longer feel what is true for ourselves. We do not really know what we want. We are living reacting to the past or preparing for tomorrow. The present moment is rarely fully received and enjoyed. We all know someone who seemingly has everything but always finds problems instead of joy. We know someone who in the middle of a joyful time begins talking about something else, for example the latest tragedy or bad news. Changing the subject brings them back to their normal serious world. Joy is difficult. We try to stay in an atmosphere that is comfortable, not too much, and not too little. Joy takes a big heart that we have not learned to inhabit. Joy inflates life with love's abundance.

*To learn to inhabit our great heart, we must make a home for our soul.*

People are just as likely to be jealous or competitive with someone who is joyful as would be an admirer and supporter. In our conversations how often do we hear someone bringing someone else down rather then wishing them well and lifting them up? The question is do they deserve their good fortune? Do we deserve joy? Joy is ok when it comes after suffering and self-sacrifice. But living a life for real food, living for joy for its own sake is threatening to everyone who believes that life is sacrifice and suffering.

The life of joy begins again as we rediscover our choices. It is the choices that we have that give us the possibility to choose joy. The root of joy, our freedom, comes from having choices. This is why two people in the same work, in similar activities or life circumstances can have entirely different experiences. Someone who feels he or she is choosing their work has a very different experience then someone who feels stuck in their work day after day. Even in difficulty, someone who finds choices in their challenges will more easily find joy versus someone who feels caught or trapped in their lives. No matter what circumstances our lives maybe in, joy comes as we begin to find choices for our awareness, choices for where we place our hearts, choices which can lead us to more honesty, peace, love, beauty, fun.

## Taking Care of Others

An example of the need for choices is when someone has a long-term illness and a close family member or friend feels they must take care of them. Caregivers and patients often suffer together from seemingly lack of choices, from damaged or destroyed passion for living. They both feel as if life gives them no alternatives. For the caregiver, when helping someone else is a sacrifice, it is not true. When helping gives joy, then it is true. For the sick and ill finding new choices is the path towards finding new hope and well-being. For the people who live in self-sacrifice, there are always many excuses. The caregiver says, "There is no one else to help. We have no money. There is no other way. "I am needed and must do my duty even if I sacrifice myself." The sick often focus on what they cannot do instead of how much of themselves they still possess. Everyday is a challenge, do they see life's limitations and lack of choices or seek joy and the choices that are still open to them?

I often ask caregivers, "If you were the one being helped, would you want someone helping you out of sacrifice or out of joy? Would you want someone to care for you by sacrificing their lives or would you want someone helping you from their love, their desire to give?" I ask the sick despite life's limitations, where can they find real food?

*Real food, the presence of fresh air, peace, love, beauty is always some-where nearby once we are willing to find new choices. Real food, one moment at a time leads to new choices, renewed passion, and joy.*

When we acknowledge choices, the solutions for finding other resources, money, support, real food begins to happen. While one person is sacrificing himself day after day giving care and having no life for himself, there may be a neighbour two doors away who is retired and looking for some value in his life. He would love to care for someone. There may be a teenager down the street who would love a little extra money and is more then ready to help. For the sick, visitors with a smile are certainly more nourishing then visitors who come out of obligation or duty. Gradually, other sources of nourishment for the heart come as well.

Finding choices is like untying a knot. We do not begin where the knot is the tightest but further away where the line is looser and can move. The choices we make before and after our times of stress change our awareness helping us to make new choices all day. Slowly, the knot itself also becomes looser and begins to untie. We need not begin where our stress is most difficult but where we can relax a little, where life is still gentle and easy. Life's knots become looser and we find more choices everywhere. Putting our hearts in the direction of looking for real food, we discover life's presence around us and within us. This is the first step to opening to life's possibilities. Regaining our passion for life is the best gift we can give ourselves. We are unfolding our soul, lifting it up from being buried underneath a life a sacrifice and suffering. The world needs love. Living anything less than our joy is to give our daily world less than what it deserves! Everyday we risk living our joy; we are giving courage to those around us to find their choices of real food, joy and to live it. No matter what circumstances our lives may be in, there are always choices of joy or fear, opening or closing to life around us and in us. Do the circumstances of our lives constrict or inspire us? Do our hearts harden or soften? Do our challenges push us to give up or to surrender to something greater, our Soul, God inside of us? Joy is opening to and receiving life's pure presence. This presence enjoys being shared with others. Living life's fullness is the best remedy for the part of us that falls down or slips into self-sacrifice, suffering, and guilt.

# Joy and Discipline

Having discipline is often confused with suffering, self-sacrifice and feeling guilty for not staying on a particular course. Joy and discipline are not opposites as most people imagine. And neither should joy and discipline necessarily be the same. The tension between a discipline, for example in athletics or academics, and feeling free in our joy helps us to get clear, to find a true path. For some the discipline in sport or academics leads to a greater joy of health, intellectual, or career development. For others the same discipline leads to feelings of self-betrayal. They are depressed for following the path given by others and not really chosen for themselves. Discipline for some is real food giving awareness to the strength of their souls. While for others the same activity may be weakening their sense of self and purpose.

*Each of us are challenged to find disciplines in life, which are true.*

Often we maintain a discipline because that is what is expected of us. Our lives are set on a certain track and we feel no choice but to stay right on course. We give little thought or more important, little heart to whether this track is really true for us. Life is easier just to continue as everyone around us expects us to continue. For many, discipline is another word for following the rules. We make compromises to keep to the path, whether it offers joy or not. In these circumstances, discipline is the mind controlling the heart, thoughts over rule what is fun, and life passes by. The calling of joy has been silenced or postponed. Unfortunately, when the date that they think they will be free arrives, more often then not, another obstacle arises. Anyone who has silenced his or her heart and feelings for so many years doesn't suddenly jump into joy. The mind continues to rule over the heart, finding obstacles, and other barriers. There is always something to do that can take priority over time to be and enjoy.

Developing the muscles of our body and mind are not to the exclusion of developing awareness of our heart and soul. It is important during these periods of life when the body and mind are working hard that our joy is not forgotten. There are always time for real food and always excuses of having too much to do. No matter what activities occupy our schedule we do not need to include a sacrifice of our hearts, our joy.

## *The Discipline of Practicing Our Truth*

Some people would say, "Joy is not acting responsibly, I have responsibilities at home and work. What about our responsibilities for our children, partners, parents?" The list goes on and on. The list is really a list about the pressures we carry and the fears we have preventing us from living fully. The list is a list of all the excuses we have to avoid joy. Of course we do have responsibilities. The question is when is enough? How much is enough? What is enough? Generally the more we see life in terms of responsibilities, the more we are without a life of joy. The more responsibilities we list the more boring and stiff we are to others and ourselves. Responsibilities and joy are not exclusive. Each day there is time for responsibilities and time for joy. It can be all too easy for life to become less and less about joy and more and more about responsibilities, which in other words is seriousness and stress. With time for joy each day, we begin to see the difference between our responsibilities and our fears, our responsibilities and our lack of caring and listening to our heart. Seriousness and responsibilities become humor and joy as we make a practice of seeking and enjoying real food each day. Slowly, slowly a life of passion is replacing a life of obligation and duty. We are remembering we are a soul. There is more to life then responsibilities. Joy and responsibility do not have to be separate. We can have great joy fulfilling our responsibilities! This is when our list of things to do is not a list of all our fears but our joy. This comes from a life that honors, seeks, and enjoys real food.

> *The true discipline maybe finding real food when we have little time or energy. Finding real food each day maybe the most important discipline, a discipline of choosing joy. The discipline of being true to one's self may be the most difficult discipline of all.*

When is the surrender of momentary joy part of building a life of greater joy? And when is the surrender of present joy part of a pattern of denying our heart in general? The discipline of practicing our truth maybe the most important discipline we acquire in life. There are so many pressures to not listen to one's feelings, to be like everyone else, to not question, to follow. It may seem easier just to continue the daily routine of sacrifice but something calls us, the longing of our souls. Something greater awaits us. There is a discipline of listening inside and finding new choices. Slowly, one fresh choice leads to another. Our soul is being heard and embraced. The path of joy gives greater strength to be true in every aspect of life. Joy is not an easy path. To be true to our joy, committed to joy, open for joy, to receive joy fully is very challenging when the soul has become buried in the heart covered over in our serious world. Discipline may begin by discovering how far away we are from our passion, fun, and simple being. Then true discipline continues seeking real food, enjoying real food, making a life that nourishes our whole being.

# II. The Daily Life

# *Joy in Relationship*

Nowhere is real food more apparent or more absent then in our partnerships and with our friends. In modern life when we carry so much of the daily world in our hearts, less and less of us is available for relationships. Many people live alone. Many more people, who live in relationship, feel as if they are alone. Our hearts are full of just about everything leaving little room for love. We offer and receive little because of the over crowding in our hearts. Relationships suffer as we suffer from our lack of joy.

Relationships are where we most easily find joy and seemingly most easily lose our joy. In our partnerships we see our joy and see where we compromise and give up our joy. Many people, who live separate from their inner river of joy, struggle for and hold tightly onto a relationship to give them what they are missing. We look for someone to give the joy we cannot find for ourselves. When we find this person it soon becomes difficult. The love is not enough or not how we want it. The other person, no matter how much they try, cannot satisfy us. For a while the relationship works but sooner or later one or both of us get tired of trying to satisfy the other.

> *When we are our source of joy, our partner can be himself or herself. They can have good days and bad days. They do not need to hide parts of themselves or try to be different to try to please us. And we can be ourselves.*

We support one another to have real food in our lives, to live our joy! In a new relationship or an old relationship beginning again, enjoying real food with one another and in one another makes the heart of the relationship.

It is beautiful to remember love's beginnings. It is here that we get glimpses of love's potential and our soul's true nature. In the beginning, falling in love is the meeting of two souls. Concerns with the daily world do not exist. In these times, only love is real. Two souls are meeting in seemingly limitless possibility. We are excited in almost every cell of our body. Love's abundance is everywhere. This is a reflection of the power and potential of our souls being fully present in our lives. When we are living our river of joy we quickly and easily say, "yes" to everything we are feeling and experiencing. With love, no obstacle seems so important or overwhelming. Love is greater than all. We discover so much energy, we can hardly sleep. When our lover leaves in the morning, we still feel their presence around us and in us.

During the day, we seem to know how they are, what they are feeling. When the phone rings we know if it is they calling. Love's wonderful being is everywhere. Rivers of energy are flowing through us. Our creativity and ideas of what is possible are opened and pouring out non-stop. If only we could turn off our minds and feel it all! If only we could stop making plans, turn off our pictures, our fantasies of the future, and simply be present. If only life could be like this forever. Our families and friends just think we are "in love". More often then not, they tell us, "not to get hurt, be careful. Be sure it is right." And sometimes we hear from those who know love, "enjoy it, play, have fun, be all you can". Meanwhile inside of us something incredible is happening. We discover feelings we never knew we had. We find prayer unfolding naturally as if saying. "May this love feed every part of my partner, everything inside that hungers. May this love be a gift for all beings." In these times it feels as if our lover, indeed everyone we meet on the street is a part of us. There is no separation. This joy is meant for everyone. We are souls. God is everywhere. Inside each of us is a loving God recognizing God in the other. In the nakedness shared with one another, love is blooming. We are amazed by how much love is moving our thoughts, feelings, changing everything in our lives.

### Dare to Live in Love's Ocean

In these times, our souls are unfolding. We think it is the relationship-taking root in our lives. But it is more. The relationship is an impulse for our souls. Love itself is finding place in our being. It is taking its place against all our fears and the skepticism and judgments of those around us. If we have been living apart from our river of joy, we are afraid of feeling too much. Falling in love, the idea is great, but the experience is unsettling or overwhelming. When our inner river of joy is shallow or covered in worldly concerns, we try to control our falling in love. The new love is usually short lived or quickly brought under some limits. We quickly try to define the relationship. What is it? Where are we going? Is this a new friend or my new partner? We make categories as an attempt to limit and hold onto the experience. In modern culture, we usually try to limit love's passion and be practical. We try to come back to normal reality. We do not trust love's waves. We do not know love's ocean. We quickly try to organize love so we are comfortable and the heart does not get too naked. The soul is briefly touched but usually not embraced for long. Soon the joy has nowhere to go inside. Fears surface. We are afraid to lose ourselves. Lovers quickly jump into making plans instead of living their newly found depths of being. They often rush to put the relationship into practical worldly limits instead of remaining open and available to where love leads them.

Love, God's gift opens us to our true nature. Our heart is open, present. Our soul is unfolding perfectly, seemingly so naturally in our lives. Love has pierced our defenses, our normal personality. Love has raised the covers hiding our hearts. Everything is exposed. Love's impulse is awakening the depths of our being. Our soul has never felt so real, so true. Surely nothing is an accident. Every moment, every encounter has purpose. What is real and what is only my imagination? Does the other really feel as I feel? Do I let go into the vastness? Is this real or a dream? Should I protect myself? Maybe it is all too much. Where are the boundaries?

When lovers or new friends meet and the special energy is honored, protected, lived as much as possible, love takes root. Trust in one's self grows with trust in the other. Our souls come forward in our hearts, in our awareness and unfold in our lives. These times include feelings of being completely understood even before or without talking. There are moments of great nakedness, acceptance, vulnerability, excitement, and fulfillment. Every part of life seemingly is leading us to more love, more aspects of our soul. We feel as if our core being has been undressed. In the nakedness of the relationship so much is present.

*These are sacred times. There is much more occurring then simply meeting a new friend or falling in love. Heaven and Earth have come together inside of us.*

Each soul is discovering places inside, a vast expanse of being, openness, purpose. There is a new kind of security that includes feelings of being completely insecure. Love itself seems to give so much including new confidence, knowing, trust, peace, a feeling of being connected with our selves, others, nature all around us. Love has penetrated the hardened places inside reminding us that we are much more. Joy seems to have an unlimited source within us. Two souls are merging and unfolding together. Or were we already merged and just didn't know it? Aren't we interwoven with everyone but too egocentric to realize it?

*Love is unfolding our essence. Love's simple being heals all kinds of separation. Joy is entering places where love has never been. Our bodies become joy's body.*

Love is making a true home not only for our partner but also for our souls in our hearts and in the world. God has become physical.

What is this love? Is it only giving? When or how much should we receive? Is love selfish or selfless? Is love possible in a world that is practical first, responsible second, with love being way down on the list? How do we keep the mystery alive? Can we drown in love and still live in this world? In our fear, the questions seem endless. In love's presence, everything is possible. There are no limits. Only in this moment is the answer. Love is lived one minute at a time. Love begins anew each day, loving the other, as they want to be loved. Yes, love is loving the other, as they want to be loved.

This giving, freely out of our joy is the building block of a strong relationship. With our children, we know this. Our joy is loving the children, as they want to be loved. Of course there are times both children and adults need to have boundaries. Every relationship needs some structure, a foundation. This structure gives the relationship safety, trust, room in which to grow. Giving a relationship a clear structure gives love a secure place to fill. Lack of structure or unclear commitment or boundaries, creates misunderstanding and lack of trust. Children and adults can spend more time arguing over boundaries instead of enjoying the relationship. Relationships with minimal clear boundaries have maximum strong joy. Relationships with maximum boundaries have limited joy. With too many boundaries, a relationship becomes a power struggle instead of a gift to be enjoyed again and again. Clarity in relationship builds strength. Relationships grow in joy, as there is safety. Safety gives trust.

*We give to each other, as we would want to be given to. Joy is in the other's face, the eyes and smile, as he or she is loved as they wish. Love is in the small things.*

## *Offering and Receiving*

Love is in the offering of our selves but it is also in the receiving. This is the balance that is often missing. Love is the opportunity to offer our selves completely and also to receive deeply. In modern life our offering is limited because we do not know how to receive. Love begins again and again by receiving the other. Couples that really receive one another offer each other unending joy. Receiving is taking the time to feel the unique presence of our partner. Receiving is to have all our senses and heart present with each other. More then listening to the words shared, more then understanding the feelings expressed, receiving is to drink the special qualities, the essence and being. Receiving is like saying a great "yes" to our partner. This "yes", this pure acceptance is food for our souls. The nourishment of the relationship, makes the challenges and obstacles we encounter smaller, and not so important. We receive, drinking the other's simple presence of beauty, their strength, their vulnerability, their grace. Receiving the other builds the foundation for the relationship. This receiving is two souls realising the oneness of being.

> *The separation we think divides us is really not true. We are separate bodies and personalities, but together in an ocean of being. In relationship, two souls are consciously letting go of separateness and being in love's ocean.*

Shared joy loves the person as they are, without conditions. However, few people know this kind of love because they never experienced it for themselves. Beginning early in childhood, we were rarely received and just loved. Very quickly we learned how to perform to do well for love. Love based on how well we perform quickly enters into relationships with each partner thinking they must do something to keep the other. Each person tries to guess what the other wants or sacrifices his or her wishes so the other is happy. Soon each is unhappy because they have given up on themselves. In the beginning the new partner is everything we always wanted and later the same partner can be everything we don't like. What has happened? We have abandoned our own river of joy trying to please the other or hoping against hope the other will give us what we need. Most relationships suffer because each feels they are not loved for just being themselves.

How do we love the other, as they want to be loved without abandoning ourselves? How do we love our partner and not leave our own river of joy? The answer begins with what is our joy? What is this love? The simple presence of our lover is our joy. To receive the presence of our partner is to feed the relationship. As we receive the presence of our lover, the details of life find a path. Many couples are too busy with managing the details of the relationship and lose contact with the relationship itself. The presence of the partner gets lost in the business of daily life. Soon two strangers are living together. All the details of job, home, children are taken care of but we do not know whom we are living with. We are taking the time for everything but have no time to receive the other. This receiving is not in what we do together. This receiving is not in the taking care of the other's needs. This receiving is in the silence that we share together. This receiving is beyond our words, beyond our activities. Receiving is having space inside us for the other.

> *To take our partner in our hearts, our being, this is the gift of relationship. To have someone who really takes us inside, appreciates us, holds us, this is relationship's joy.*

To be with the other, to feel their life, their work, their joys, their hopes and disappointments, this is receiving. Receiving is being together underneath all the chores of life. Love is going down to the river in each of us and going further into the ocean of being together. When we look into each other's eyes we are looking into the ocean of life's presence. This is the true relationship, sharing life's simple presence.

## *Childhood Patterns in Adult Relationships*

In the search for love, we often choose someone to take care of. We think, if we sacrifice ourselves for them, they will do the same for us. At an early age, we tried to take care of Mother's or Father's needs and wishes. As children we were rewarded for what we did or how well we performed. Love was more about behaving a certain way then receiving the simple love of no conditions. As adults, we try to be the perfect partner. We do everything correctly. We try to take care of the other the best we can. We perform and do everything hoping to find the love we are missing. As children no matter what we did or how well we performed, we did not get the love we wanted. And as adults, we still do not find the love we are seeking. We give up ourselves, our joy, again and again thinking there is some kind of trade or bargaining for love. We feel alone in relationship and without.

Some of us as children rebel and get in all kinds of trouble. We noticed the trouble we get into also gets parental attention. The attention is exciting, not very loving but at least it is attention. As adults we continue. We are the partners that are not available, that disappoints again and again. The "good" child finds the "bad" child and tries to change them. Often in relationships, we pick someone we think we can love and fix or heal. Then everything will be okay. Meanwhile, we are hoping and then disappointed time and again. All kinds of patterns for love are tried as children and tried again as adults. Some people find someone to notice them and to take care of them. They hope the love they want will stay. Others look for someone to love and take care of but the new partner takes the attention for granted and expects more and more.

We enter relationships unhappy and think the new relationship will make our lives different. Or we enter into relationships happy and often find ourselves suffering not too long afterwards. What happens? One day we are happy sharing our joy together with our new friend and soon we are struggling to keep the connection and become disappointed. Where did the joy go? Or more accurately, when did we abandon our selves, our river of joy? Often we quickly leave or lose our own feelings, our truth, the river of joy because we do not live it well ourselves. We try to satisfy and meet the expectations of the other and lose our selves in the process. The new partner meanwhile is doing the same, abandoning him or herself trying to keep the relationship together. Each of us has our own river to be in. How can leaving our joy serve the other? Of course, we cannot keep someone else in his or her joy. They must follow their course. We meet, joining together again and again. A true relationship is an abundance of shared joy.

> *The mystery of relationship opens again and again as we remember it is not what we do for each other. It is not what we do together. Love is not the activities and possessions we share. It is not a meeting of the minds. Love's mystery is in the presence of love. It is the windows of the heart that open when we are together.*

It is the communion, gentleness, understanding, peace, and joy we discover. The relationship is much more then what we say. It is more then our likes and dislikes, more then the feelings we have in common. The true relationship is learning to enjoy the presence of the relationship itself. Love is the innocence, trust, passion, devotion, and gratitude we feel when we are with each other. It is two people receiving the wonder of the other, joy's presence in the other. This is the bond that holds two people together. No matter how far apart two people become, the moment one begins to receive the other, to let the presence of the other touch them, be with them, the relationship begins again.

## Saying "Yes" to Each Other

In difficult times, sometimes we may think a new partner would be better. But what is really happening is that two souls are no longer touching the beauty and joy in each other. Joy may be easier at least in the beginning with someone new. But we still have our own challenge to live a life of real food. This includes learning to enjoy the real food in our partner. Whoever our partner is, we still have to learn to be true to our river and receive the river of the other. Differences of personalities, likes and dislikes have little influence when souls are receiving and enjoying one another.

> *Love is receiving the very best in each other. Love is being patient with everything human in ourselves and our partner.*

May be the same difficulties we find in this partner, we will find with another. The parts of the other we do not like can be as much our problem as theirs. What we do not like about ourselves or about life, we often see in those closest to us. What we are most critical of and judgmental about, we often find and then focus on, in those living with us. The people we love the most, we can be the harshest with. Commitment begins with being true to our own river. This gives our partner the space and support to embrace his or her unique life of joy. Commitment is each coming deeper into our river meeting again and again in the great ocean of being, of relationship. This is a true relationship. Instead of making our partner our excuse for us not finding our joy, relationship calls us down to the river until we surrender to God's gift, unfolding our soul in our lives.

Partnership is making each other bigger. This means seeing and supporting one another to be more ourselves, to be creative, powerful, joyful in the world. True relationships are as if saying a big "yes" to one another. Each feels more of their potential, life's possibilities. This "yes" is to help keep the wonder and joy of love's beginnings. "Yes" keeps love growing. "Yes" supports each to continue opening to and expressing our soul in our life. Partnership is not an excuse to remain as we are or to make the other smaller. The bigger, more passionate, more successful, more joyful one becomes is a gift for the partner to expand as well. There are all kinds of new places inside the heart for both to be touched and explore. This leads to all kinds of new opportunities to experience and express our hearts in the world.

So often couples become fixed on what they want to change in the other instead of receiving the shelter of two souls living together. This shelter supports each person to reach further into his or her inner recourses. This shelter supports each to risk more, to be vulnerable, free, and powerful in the world. Shelter, allows one or both partners to do less in the world and be more with themselves, the journey of their soul. In a busy world, the shelter of relationship protects our innocence, our playful being. Personalities have softened, surrendered to discover two souls are one. This joining of rivers is very special. Each is made bigger, more complete. Two rivers have come together to discover the vast ocean within. Relationships fifty years old or new, realise love's beginnings are never far away. The excitement, the mountains of creativity and life's possibilities are here. A true relationship is new after every encounter, every meeting.

Family, partner, friends, each relationship is unique. A relationship is more then two people sharing some activity, our thoughts and feelings. There is a spirit to each relationship. The spirit forms a bond, touching, connecting two people. Each relationship is an impulse to discover new richness of our soul. The spirit of each relationship provides shelter, an experience of wholeness, and special nourishment. When the relationship is not recognised and freshly received, the spirit withdraws and goes away. A relationship, as each of us, needs real food to thrive. With nourishment, the spirit takes hold in our hearts and grows in our lives.

Most people leave a relationship to develop by chance. The potential is rarely realised. People get distracted, drift apart. Often two people find themselves just living together. Many relationships fall apart because the spirit is not appreciated. The relationship is not given real food.

Love needs to be fed. Real food for relationships is found when two people slow down in the enjoyment of life's intimate being.

> *Real food is in the silence in the midst of our activity. Real food is sharing the sacredness of life including the sacredness of one another.*

Struggling partners so easily forget that relationships are gifts to be opened again and again. The spirit of each relationship touches a special part of our soul. A relationship can never be repeated or duplicated. When a relationship is not received, the spirit dries up and goes away. One day the relationship is over. To find, renew, or build a relationship, our souls must call and receive the spirit. The spirit of a relationship is greater then our thoughts and feelings. It is something much more then the emotions that push and pull us. Golden threads are weaving together in and out, and through each soul. Each is becoming more in the presence of the other. Real food makes the gold more golden. New colors are always flowing into the tapestry of the relationship. The unique spirit of each relationship calls for our attention, devotion, and appreciation. Each relationship is a special kind of joy that nourishes our soul.

# *Joy in Work*

Like relationships, work is also where we can easily find or lose our joy. Work is much more then how we make money. It is where we can discover life's passion, creativity, and truth. We often think joy begins the day when we no longer have to work. We believe it is normal for work to be separate from joy. Who says we should enjoy our work? When we work without joy, we usually do not know what to do with our free time. We live with little or no joy. We do not know how to live the simple joys now and probably will not later when we retire. The duty, the burdens, the seriousness of work hangs over men and now more and more women who have joined the men's joyless world of work. Men and women are nearly equals in being toughened, hardened, and saddened by the lack of joy in their lives. Eight hours a day, five days a week, month after month, they are nearly equals in their separateness from their joy, their souls. Men and women are leaving their hearts at home while they go to work, hoping to find time for their hearts later.

> *We work instead of live. We work more and more and live less and less. Some of us think, more work or new work is the answer. But what we need is to learn how to live.*

Work does not need to be separate from life! Even the wealthy are often wealthy in everything but their joy, their passion. Many of us do not have to work so much or work at all but continue to do so. We suffer a loss of purpose and direction if not working. Joy is a scary, vulnerable path. What would we do if we do not stay busy? To learn to be true to our joy, in what we do to earn an income, is the next frontier of modern business and economy.

Work is truly satisfying when it comes from our creative source. Our creative source is our river of joy. Joy's calling is work that deeply satisfies. This work is not only in what we are doing but also in the relationships at work, the environment of our work. Joy's presence can be in everything connected with work. Customers who feel listened to, appreciated, loved, return to be customers again. Products that were made from love have qualities that attract people to buy them. An environment of love makes people want to come back and be there again and again. Work that is an expression of our joy becomes a magnet, a meeting place, a success, because joy is success. Success is an expression of our joyful journey. True success comes from our souls. Success can mean lots of money or not. Satisfying work is not a process towards a goal. The process itself is joyful, meaningful, and fulfilling.

In work as in relationships, there are many temptations to abandon our river. We compromise for security. We are afraid to risk. There are always doubts that our joy can actually make a living. Step by step, one day a week, part time, full time we slowly grow into a life of joy, a life that is unfolding our soul. This process of step by step includes our work as well. Most people if suddenly given their ideal working situation would not know what to do with it. They would find problems and insecurity instead. Similarly, most people even if they find the perfect partner they will find something wrong, some excuse to deny the love. They are not prepared for their souls, to live abundantly in joy's world.

Slowly, slowly real food allows our joy to grow and take root in our lives. Real food nourishes our passion, our creativity. A few minutes of real food each day, gives us the inspiration, courage, strength, the well being to be our joy. Then we begin naturally expressing our joy. We do what feels right. It comes from our whole being. What we do in the world expresses our true nature. When we feel and honor our joy, finding friends, activities, work that affirm our essence, our true nature follows. As joy takes root in our being, joy becomes more and more natural in every part of our day. We see from experience that joy's river runs over obstacles, around them, and sometimes right through them. Why should joy in work be any different or more difficult then joy in relationship or life in general? Why do we assume work is work without joy?

## *Being Successful*

Finding our true work and finding our joy is one in the same. Following our river of joy, the money flows. Success is much more then in how much we have and how much we do. Success is the dance of our soul in the world. Success is staying up to the middle of the night working on a project, having long ago forgotten or caring what time it is. Success is the heart pumping wildly with creativity. Success is in the little moments of beauty each day. It is making others happier, lives easier, hearts fuller. Success is being able to be honest with everyone you are working with. Success is being trusted to take a day or two days off. Success is how the universe responds to a good idea. And the good ideas just keep coming. Success is our true nature. Success comes from our souls because our souls are success.

In true work you can see the joy. It is in the faces, the quality of the product, the atmosphere where we are working. It is in way people are listening and being with one another. Working from our soul is bringing love in to the world each in our own way. Working from joy means much less worry and much more fun. Work is fun! Good work is lots of fun! What is more important to bring into the world besides joy? And if we do not know and practice joy, how do we expect to give this to others? Imagine, all the hours, days, weeks, months, years in needless worry transformed to joy? Instead of being mountains of stress, we are rivers of joy, simplicity, peace, and success. This is our true work. We are called to work at becoming rivers of peace. This is a good work.

This is remembering who we are. This is risking and finding true success!

If the birds in the air and the animals on the ground find food, why shouldn't we? How much energy do we find for worrying about what to eat and where we will sleep instead of enjoying life?

> *The vast majority of our worries are not really about how we make a living but how separate we are from ourselves. Worries about money are worries about how insecure we are separated from our well of being.*

How can we be successful in life if our feelings, our passion, our hearts are turned off eight hours a day? The new frontier in business is to have joy where we make a living. This is what makes a truly strong economy, unleashing infinite possibilities of joy in what we do to make money.

Joyful work begins with having time for real food each day. Slowly the knots in our thinking loosen opening our life at work to new possibilities. The people we think are against us or at least not with us, also want joy. Everyone can win. As we nourish our hearts outside of work, we begin to recognize the presence of real food at work. Instead of reacting to the difficulty in any situation or the worst in someone at work, we find ourselves reaching for the best of each situation and everyone around us. Instead of limitations of what we thought, we see new what is possible. Joy softens the heart in us and everyone else. Everyone is looking for a way out of the life of our fears to the sunshine. The sunshine is the brilliance of our souls.

# Our Soul Mate, Work, and Destiny

While others search for their true partner or work, we practice living our river of joy. Life is less of a search and more a practice of being. The right partner and work is a natural extension of unfolding our souls. The perfect partner and work come from finding our own perfect joy. We are not looking in the world for someone or some work to complete us. Partnership and work come from our essence and being. They are expressions of our joy.

Our partner is more then our husband or wife. Work is more then where we make an income.

> *Our partner and work are extensions of our own true being. They are part of our soul being and unfolding in this life.*

They are a part of us and they are gifts given to us. Our partner and work are real food to receive fresh everyday. As long as we are separated from ourselves, from our joy, we cannot find our soul mate, our true work, our destiny. We are always looking outside ourselves and are left with feelings of disappointment. Even when we find someone special or a work that looks promising, we are doubtful. We find something missing. We find something to struggle with. Without having our inner joy, anything found outside is never enough. All we know is how to live separate, separate from life's joy. We are expecting something to go wrong because inside we are not use to living what it true. No one or no work can bring us into our river except our own efforts. Thus many people give up on having a partnership. They work and work and work until retirement. Unfortunately many are also giving up on the calling of joy!

The path is in the choices that we make everyday. Do we take time for ourselves and nourish our deeper being? Are we living with real food, community, and activities that give something genuine to our lives? Can we let go enough of life's daily demands including our fears to come inside ourselves? Can we feel our own presence coming from our soul? In our own well of peace, we naturally find God. We naturally find others who have found this part of themselves. We are soul mates. We are spiritual family on the path of eternity. From our source of creativity and passion, we naturally find our work. Listening to and honoring our talent we find work with heart in it. Work has heart because we are using our talent, which comes, out of our joy. Work flows out of our inner resources, our truth, our enjoying of others, and our service to the world. Our lives are joyful because we are honoring our own life force, our being.

Even if our partner is a soul mate, they still have a personality, likes and dislikes that may or may not match our own. We still have disappointments and behavior and emotions that are not always easy to live with. We are still very human. However, if we are living in our soul's world, joy's way, these are not great obstacles. Living in our own river, we can enjoy the river of the other. Two become truly one as we make a life for our souls. The separation we feel from our partner is also the separation we have from ourselves. The union we find with another is just as much union we have with our own wholeness. Our commitment to joy is support for everyone in our lives to be more and unfold their souls.

In joy's path there is no question that we have a soul and our soul has a destiny. There is only the practice of being true to ourselves, which keeps us in our ocean of well being. Our destiny is always manifesting.

When we are living joy's river, we do not need signs, teachers, or some authority to tell us what to do, how to live, when this or that will happen. The story of our lives is not as important as love's presence. Our soul's destiny is not in what we do or possess but in our ocean of being and service to others. We are not called to be important but to be ourselves. We are not going somewhere special but being more and more special where we are. In this moment is our soul's destiny. Relationships and work take on new meaning. Our soul mate and work are natural extensions of our joy, our soul unfolding in the world.

# Spirituality, Religion, and Joy

Traditionally religion by its very nature was real food. The ritual and prayers would touch people daily and remind them of their soul and God. Temple or church was a place to feel connected to ourselves, each other, to the sacred. Today many religions are more about doctrine and control then about love and joy. The soul and God is more of a matter of belief rather then personal experience. Today for many, religion fails to awaken our awareness of being a soul and a child of God.

Children are naturally alive in the beauty of God's abundant love. Children easily embrace life, God, and forgiveness. Traditionally religion was to provide a shelter for being God's child. Generation after generation, we are reminded of God's presence in every aspect of life. The presence of our ancestors is remembered. Religion is to remind everyone of the path of their soul, life's gifts, and joy's presence. The purpose of church is to remind us to build a living church inside of us. The living church frees us from this world to our life in eternity. The living church is a shelter to let go of our struggles and remember the joy, God's presence inside of us and in the world.

For many people the modern church is no longer living. With its emphasis on God being outside of our own being, religion leaves us feeling more separation instead of less. God as some distant being is difficult to approach and know. Religion can become an inner battle of feeling deserving or undeserving of life's joys. Life becomes a course, at times against our nature and wishes, hoping this will bring us rewards. We forget to remember God as being something we have to open to in our hearts and receive. God as a universal presence of love becomes unknown. Many religious leaders, feeling little spirit themselves, are busy with complicated theology, missing simple kindness and generosity. When God is projected outside of us, it is only natural we become judgmental of others and distant from our own spirit and joy.

## *Finding God Inside of Us*

Religion, reminding us that God is inside, a part of us, our very soul, is very different. How can we know God in one another, in the world, and great cosmos if we do not appreciate and know God in ourselves? This is where the separation begins. Intellectuals and philosophers have been talking about this separation for centuries. Meanwhile, the simple people, the mystics, everyone who lives God's joy everyday, have no problem believing, loving, surrendering, and devoting themselves to God. This is as normal as life itself.

> *God is life itself. He, She is intertwined in all that we are and do. When religion reminds us of our inner beauty, love, gentleness, truth, humility, innocence, and giving nature, God is not very far away and neither is joy.*

Our separation from God and joy are one and the same. Those who rediscover joy's ways know God as the water and source of all life. When religion teaches God as something outside of us it requires a belief in God. When religion reminds us of God's beauty and joy inside of us, no belief is necessary. We are the heart, hands, eyes, and mouth of God. Like the joy of children and the birds in early morning flight, joy is God's presence in the world.

In our modern culture, there is great pressure upon religion or anyone that teaches development of the heart. People want something that is practical. In our intellectual world, there is very little support to discuss anything about the heart but in the terms of science. Everyone knows the heart is a pump for our blood. Very few know our heart as the home of our soul. Modern religion teaches about the soul in mostly abstract terms. When we live in a culture where our awareness is more in thought than being, more in doing than enjoying, it is no surprise the soul is hidden and difficult to know.

Today, the energy in many churches feels similar to the energy in shopping centers, schools, and other public buildings. The same mental energy for shopping, studying, and sports is in our churches as elsewhere. Most people do not know the difference. They do not know the presence of devotion, prayer, and ritual. They do not recognize the sweetness of sacredness that fills the heart and the room around us in heartfelt prayer and meditation. The knowledge and appreciation of sacredness is becoming lost. Not so long ago, the center of most cities and villages was the town church. Daily life was centered around spirituality and community. Today the center of our cities is skyscrapers or sports arenas. Secular activity has replaced the journey of remembering where we come from and the life in eternity.

It is no wonder that complex theology has replaced simple joy, forgiveness, and service to those who are in need. Religion that is not about feeling and opening the heart by definition is going to be dry and leave us feeling separate. When prayer and ritual become routine without including the heart, religion becomes form without substance. It is no accident that joy and our souls remain unknown. We cannot blame the church for forgetting to remind us of the path back to God. The thinking in modern religion mirrors modern thinking in general.

God remains an intellectual question because this is the culture we live in. The joy children naturally feel about God is often pushed in the background with stories of guilt, suffering, and sacrifice. Joy's reservoir, the abundance of God inside and around the children is unrecognized. We fail to remind them of their natural beauty, being, devotion, gentleness, service, and gratitude. We fail to teach the practices of the heart that keep God's presence and their pure being close to them. People everywhere are looking for the specific steps to reenter their heart's sanctuary. They want to remember their souls. And these steps are not being taught. Instead of remembering our failings, imagine church or temple reminding us to remember our joy and the many gifts of life we are given. Joy, our inner ocean, is forgotten because priests and ministers do not know their own joy and inner sanctuary. Religion has forgotten its roots in the great love in the examples of Christ, Mary, the masters, prophets, saints, great teachers, and mystics. The mind cannot teach love.

> *Only the heart illuminates the hearts in others.*

## Psychology Without Heart

Modern culture, in particular, psychology, is for many the new religion. With no belief in God, the self is pursued. But what is the self that we are pursuing? Our self is more then modern education. It is more then fulfilling our desires and being comfortable. It is more then studying how our thinking influences our behavior. We are more then our thoughts and emotions. Inside of us is much more then our anger and pain. Modern psychology usually fails to include a renewal of self-acceptance, innocence, play, passion, trust, our inner well of being. God inside of us and in the world is all but ignored. For most of us, modern psychology does not open the doors to the life of joy. It is trapped in the small rooms of our intellect and emotions.

> *Changing our behavior is no substitute for living our joy. Turning to chemicals, taking a daily pill, is no substitute for discovering who we are and unfolding our soul.*

People are depressed, suffering, living alone because of their separation from their inner source. This inner source is their joy, God's intimate presence. In psychology, generally the many spaces in our hearts are left unexplored. Our lightness of being, inner peace, and love, which are God inside of us, are not included. The focus on our thoughts and emotions leaves out our greater awareness. The focus on our behavior and what is behind our actions does not acknowledge the other parts of us. Our pure being, need for solitude, generosity of spirit, capacity of compassion and surrender are not supported.

As modern psychology untangles our childhood events a greater peace is already with us. As therapists try to change behavior, they often do not see and remind their clients of the beauty within and around them. Thoughts and feelings are analysed or expressed as life's pure presence and simple peace stand humbly by.

> We are more than our thoughts and feelings. Many rooms in our heart call out for our attention. Our well of deep being, remains hidden and covered.

There is little understanding or intention to remember and re-enter this reservoir of being which includes the many joys of the heart. Children naturally know their inner reservoir. They naturally live from joy's inner abundance until it is slowly or abruptly closed down within them. This happens when their inner world is unrecognised and unsupported. The seriousness and demands of the daily world close down joy's spaciousness inside. The world of God and spirituality, so normal in other cultures, soon becomes mostly an abstraction.

Meanwhile, therapy is about the daily world of relationships and emotions. Most therapists do not integrate spirituality with psychology. We do not understand that joy is the bridge! When we do not remember our own innocence, we cannot remind others. When we do not rest in our own pure spirit, we cannot guide others. Meanwhile our compromises, conflicts, daily stress are calling for joy. And this joy comes from having real food in our life. Joy comes from going inside our self, embracing our thoughts and feelings and going beneath them to our well of being.

## *Embracing Ourselves Completely*

Today in most temples and churches, it is much the same. Religion makes our own thoughts and feelings unimportant or at worst, wrong. We often separate from ourselves, our joy and try to be who we think the church tells us to be. Often, special parts of our identity, particularly our feelings and desires, are cut off as we try to be someone else. There can be a denial of our natural way of being in relationships and in the world. When is the last time we heard a priest or minister say, "God is love! To know this love, we must embrace our hearts, who we are everyday. We must embrace ourselves completely. We are called to honor our creativity, our sexuality, the parts of us that are small and those that are large. Every part of us is a gift worthy of our gratitude." Instead most churches have an agenda of being something other then ourselves, being correct and right in the eyes of others. We become rigid, judgmental, and dry of passion for life. We are not remembering the spirit, our beauty that we brought into the world. We are not remembering the sanctuary of our hearts.

When we are more devoted to a set of beliefs then listening inside, when we are busier with discipline then being true to our hearts, life becomes dry, our river is barren. We may think we are becoming free of feelings, going beyond this world. But in truth we are becoming distant from ourselves, our precious river of life, God's ocean of rich being inside. We are living in mental worlds separated from our joy, heart, and soul. We are separated from God's beauty in the world all around us.

> *Religion, for many is a struggle between our small self and divine self. Without joy healing our separation, we think one thing, feel another, and behave another. Life is disconnected.*

When we feel disconnected, it is easy to believe God is about suffering and religion is about sin and sacrifice. When God is not found inside, it is no surprise that prayer and meditation do not make life's difficulties go away. Appearances of a religious life do not help us with our inner conflicts. Anger can easily turn into self-importance. Religious correctness can cover much pain and doubt inside. The river of life, sexuality, desires, all kinds of feelings have nowhere to go. In all religion there is not much support for our human limits. What do we do with our small self, which comes again and again despite the teachings? People learn to hide their behavior in some places while living it somewhere else. They feel wrong for having difficulties, sexual feelings or for being ill. After years of following a certain path, they no longer trust and believe in themselves. They are afraid of being on their own. Many people become reconciled with being two separate people, one person in church and another at home. There are the Divine moments, filled with the grace. And then comes again and again our normal self with all our moods and problems. We can make all kinds of excuses. We pray, meditate, live the prescribed lifestyle, follow all rules, but inside we are much the same, dry and searching. Nearly everyone thinks his or her church has the truth. Meanwhile, most every church suffers the same modern problems too much talking and not enough love.

The problem in modern psychology and most religions is they become a rational for life's suffering and not a path for remembering, rediscovering life's beauty, creativity, and freedom. Religion is more often a place where we give up to some authority rather than finding our own truth. We surrender ourselves to others and rules and what we are told, instead of surrendering to God in our own hearts. The life of joy is more than something that comes from therapy, reading Holy books and following other's directions.

> *Joy is vulnerability, innocence, spontaneity, trust, beauty, and love. Joy's path believes in our selves, trusting our feelings, listening to our own truth.*

Psychology and religion have difficulty encouraging us to find our own inner truth, God inside. When therapists or ministers have their own joy, they are immediately understood. They are speaking directly from their hearts to the heart in us all. And no matter what therapy they practice or what religion they come from, the message is always clear. Life is wonder-full. Joy is who we are! Without joy, life is without real fruit!

In psychology and all religions, everyone who makes a sincere journey into their hearts find joy, lots of joy. Others can think about joy, study it, argue with it, and debate about the life of joy. But only those who are willing to surrender to joy, to make joy happen, to accept the joy within them, will find the treasure. The lives of the mystics in all religions are bursting with twinkling eyes and hearts full of joy's treasures. The lives of the mystics fill the pages of Holy Books. They call everyone who is lost in the complicated world to remember the life of simple joy. The mystics of all religions who have been humbled by experiencing the great light and vast peace of our Creator know God is in and beyond all religions. At best, religion can remind us to focus and open our hearts to the infinite presence.

## *Life Without Religion?*

Meanwhile, many people are leaving traditional religion for modern life. They have had enough of old ideas, controlling leaders, and rigid standards, which are intolerant of others. They have had enough of religion that seems to deny life, passion, sexuality, and joy. But in their departure they may be also leaving their potential for a spirit full life. When life is only about our personal story, we are captive in our separateness and the superficial worlds of what we do and have.

> *We live in only mental worlds without substance, many rooms in the heart are left unexplored. To limit ourselves to modern psychology is to not see our mystical nature, the sky, stars, and great sun on the outside*

*and within us. The healing presence of silence and the sacred can remain unknown.*

Where in modern life is there support to feel the presence of God? Where else will we hear the word "soul"? When we leave religion with no alternative where will we experience the freeing process of surrender? To let go of one's self, to surrender is an important part of remembering. Without religion, who will remind us to let go of all the details of daily life and feel the quiet heart? Where will we be reminded to let go of our self-importance and feel our nakedness as the doorway to prayer and meditation?

When our temples and churches become empty, where in modern life can we go and find shelter? Just living in the busy world of buying and consuming, doing and achieving is not enough. It is within the world's great religions that we find the invitation to take refuge, find protection in community and within ourselves. Traditionally the church or temple is to provide shelter to the poor, sick, injured. This includes the poor in heart, the sick and injured spirit that we all have from time to time. A natural human need is to have community to welcome us, to come and be loved as we are. The soul yearns for a place where can we give up our roles in the world and be just ourselves.

A part of us feels wrong when we are left to pursue God in our own way. As if pushed out of church, people leaving tradition to find God and joy on their own miss the timeless ways followed by their ancestors. Remembering our ancestors, our traditions, can heal the separations we have with the past, the souls of loved ones. This remembering can open the love and gifts of our ancestors within us. The ocean of our ancestors can support us to remember we are not alone. Together we are all in the ocean of God's being.

## *Stop Struggling With the Church of Our Childhood*

Staying in struggle with the church of our childhood, limits our growth as a spiritual adults. We can receive the most spiritually when we stop fighting the struggles with the church of our childhood. As it is important to let go of the struggle with our parents so our adult partnership can grow, it is important to let go of our struggle with the church of our childhood, so we can build a new living church, a true relationship with our soul and God. Every church and teacher is limited by his or her own lack of joy. Rigidity, controlling rules, and fear begin here. The church has no more heart then the people within it. Healing our relationship with the church of our childhood is an important step in saying "yes" again to renewing religion and letting joy be our guide to a heart full life for our soul.

# III. Inner Steps

# *Remembering*

Joy or God is not something new we have to learn. The path is a way of remembering. Different than learning a new language, it is in our joyful nature. Joy is natural. God is in our remembering our original being, remembering who we were before words. The path is recollecting joys lost and now found again. God is an awareness of one's wholeness, an ancient yet innocent knowing. This remembering is a collecting of scattered parts of one's self. The way is coming home again, coming inside from life's many seasons, the cultural winds and storms that took us away from ourselves. This joy is as close as remembering to feel our breath in this moment. And this joy can be as far away as loved ones passed away but mysteriously still with us. Finding joy's way does not require us to worry about where to go, where to turn, what to do. It is remembering. Inside this remembering, the strings of awareness bring back memories, experience, and the joy of being. As the small joys are found again, life's real fruits are found more and more easily, automatically. Joy is here. Joy is not some place we have to travel to. Joy is in our own energy. God is inside of us. Remembering is rediscovering our natural being. The path of living one's joy awakens something inside, which is deeper then happiness, greater than pleasure, more substantial than comfort.

This remembering is a renewal. We are washing away thoughts and feelings that keep us separate from this simple moment. We are renewing, freeing the thoughts and the senses to be open again. Remembering is like a muscle being used again, stretched and exercised. With practice, remembering is a daily way of being which keeps awareness fresh and light. Remembering unloads the judgments and difficulties we carry for the open softness of our simple being.

### Remembering to Remember

There are many kinds of remembering. As some people find themselves playing a bad memory over and over or repeating a list of things to do, joy's way can be keeping a song or a mantra in our awareness. This replaying a moment of life's beauty keeps us in the direction of joy. It can be a prayer of God's presence chanted silently. Or simply a remembering the nakedness of this moment keeps the muscle of our awareness open and gentle. There are many doors to finding the blessings in the present moment. We are remembering, recollecting treasures in the world that reflect parts of ourselves. These parts have been scattered through our world through time, lost in childhood, broken in relationships, forgotten in dreams left behind. There is so much of ourselves to remember. Religion, ritual, prayer, are ancient paths still practiced today to remember. We are remembering whom we were when we came into the world. And remembering is also remembering to be present now. Now, every moment, each conversation, every event can be part of the great rediscovery. Joy is being found in all its subtle and grand ways.

This remembering may begin by recounting our last time of pure joy and the time before that and time before that. What does joy feel like? Remembering past joys can be a new awakening to life, our passion, and our joy now. Living joy is easier then remembering how to ride a bicycle. We can be eighty, seventy, fifty, thirty, or seventeen but joy is never very far away. There is always a part of us that is still two, four, eight, twelve, and sixteen. Joy has no age. Joy has no limited lifetime. The reservoir of joy's memories is stored within us. In our remembering we are releasing the energy of joy back into our awareness, rejuvenating our whole being.

There are many, many ways of remembering. Childhood events, teenage passions, recent moments of great beauty or fun are all stored within us. Remembering can simply be closing one's eyes briefly to all activity and being inside the heart with simple breath. Remembering can be remembering the ground under our feet while letting go of excess activity and entanglements around us. Any practice, which helps us to embrace simple being, is a form of remembering.

> *Remembering is reaching further into the heart of the moment, the conversation, the heart of being in each relationship.*

New love, great teachings, can be an impulse for this remembering. Silence and sacred places can also be impulses for us to remember the sacred parts of ourselves. People we meet and hardly know yet who deeply touch us are reminding us. Perhaps we knew them before in lives, now lost and forgotten. Perhaps their light and essence is an impulse to remember more of our own essential being. Each relationship, event, special experience in the world can be an impulse for us to remember more. It is important to receive this impulse, let it be, and go further inside of us. Much more then a meeting, activity, a new relationship is happening. We are invited to feel deeply, listen to our intuition, and receive what is being touched. We are remembering. It is important to take the time for the impulse to open and bring us more of ourselves. We are taking the time to remember our soul.

Some may think joy's way is avoiding the stress of modern life. But why would one want to live in the middle of modern day stress? Too many people are lost in the business of life that has blinded them from this moment of simple joy. In truth the stress of modern life touches us all deeply. There is no way around it. Our hearts hurt. The noise and violence around us affect us everyday. Joy's path is committed to remembering our silent nature, the presence of the soul inside, and in everyone. This remembering helps the world to also remember and value the soul. We take refuge in remembering. In our awareness is all the protection, security, guidance, and possibility of life's joy.

# Offering And Receiving

Offering and receiving is the necessary balance to a life of doing, planning, and much activity. The worldly self is not enough for a contented heart.

> *To be able to let go and surrender our daily struggles and simply be is essential to living fully.*

When we can offer or let go what routinely occupies our thoughts, we find the larger river of our being. Normally in the river of life, our attention is on our boat, our physical life. We are focused on what we, and the boats around us, are doing. For most of us, our physical life fills our attention. When we can offer this focus, our awareness goes to something else. We feel the river itself. This is offering. We are reminded of the presence of simple being. This practice of offering, normal in other cultures, has been lost in modern life.

## Offering Our Outward Identity

In modern culture, we do not know how to separate ourselves from what we routinely identify with. It is hard to imagine ourselves separate from what we do, have, and normally think about. Our normal self is attached to all these things. Offering is to experience our simple presence, our essence, who we are without all the activity. There are few places in our culture where we can practice this. We are afraid. Questions arise. "Offer to whom or what? How do we give our self away? What is left if I am not my normal activity and thoughts?"

The answers come as we let go of our thoughts about our daily activity and rest inside, in our inner being. With practice, we offer our worldly life as we connect our awareness to something else, simple being. It can be as easy as closing one's eyes momentarily to the world and resting inside, in our inner river. It is the practice itself that answers our questions. Without offering, we do not know the other parts of our self, which are greater, then our usual identity. Offering shows us our vast being in the silence. Instead, collectively and individually, we hold on to what we do, have, and think about. Everyone is independent, responsible, and separate. Our separateness grows and our trust in ourselves, one another, and life diminishes. We feel unconnected with our own inner river, God in and around us. Life is a load on our shoulders, heavy in our hearts, complicated and often lonely. People try sports and exercise or parties and vacations to forget their troubles. But forgetting temporarily is not the same as experiencing the part of us that is free of concerns, connected to something greater inside of us and in life. Through offering, we actually become free, lighter inside. Our difficulties become more a part of our worldly life and less a weight to carry inside of us. We do not identify with them so much. It is important in the modern world to understand how to know our selves, to experience our hearts apart from the world around us. We are used to keeping every conversation during the day with us. We carry our work home. We fall asleep and wake up with our worries. We hold onto our troubles as baggage always in our hands and on our backs. We do not know how to leave them. The constant motor of thoughts running through us, we think is natural. When in fact our lack of simple peace is from losing the knowledge how to offer.

The offering we make, makes room for our inner home of peace. Taking time to offer our worldly self, helps move aside life's details that pile up. Work is left at work. Life's concerns are for the appropriate place and time. Everything moves aside at least temporarily. Offering is a reminder we are something more. We are a soul. Life includes God's presence. Our practice of offering brings us back to life's essence.

## *Freeing, Clearing Our Hearts*

Offering is relieving the over crowding of our hearts. In modern life, our minds are often separate from our hearts with our thoughts distant from our feelings. This leaves our hearts separated from our soul.

> *Our soul is buried underneath everything we carry in our hearts. The busy mind is just the overflow from our busy heart. When the heart is soft and quiet, the mind becomes silent and peaceful.*

Meanwhile, it is normal to carry worries and concerns, desires and expectations, all the noise of the world in our hearts. The day's stress easily covers life's simple, pure presence. The concerns that occupy us keep our minds active and our inner beauty and well of being out of reach. The soul needs space in the heart to unfold in. This is the purpose of offering. We are emptying the heart of worldly things so there is room for our greater being.

> *Healing the mind begins in the heart.*

To know God we do not need therapy or special knowledge. Our awareness, however, is limited by the over crowded and complicated heart which grows into a judgmental and un open mind. Just as we bathe everyday, the heart too needs to be cleansed in order to experience the parts of us which are much more.

Our vast being is easily hidden or pushed down inside under our struggles. The heart can be heavy with unforgiven relationships and unresolved feelings. The heart can be easily full of little fears leaving no path for our soul to unfold. There is no space for God, no room inside for solitude, innocence, and simple joy. Our offering keeps a part of us clear of the mental traffic. For joy, the heart must be available. Each day we need to set aside some time. We want to offer, to let go of everything we are carrying and find again our simple being. Letting go and letting be, we are doing less and being more. The heart must have space for the Divine to find us and for us to find the Divine.

Offering is similar to devotion. Devotion frees the whole heart. To let our hearts pour out to God inside of us and to God in the world is to let our hearts be bathed in pure waters. There is no bath more cleansing. Devotion, so normal in other cultures has been lost in our modern way of thinking. What devotion is left is that which we feel towards our children, partner, and work. But these are just small reminders of the power and beauty of devotion's potential. Devotion can be as simple as sitting with a symbol of God and offering everything we feel inside. Devotion can be felt towards the gift of life itself as we do simple chores, prepare a meal or a garden. Work can be devotion. Relationships can be devotion to God in one another. Devotion is taking the time for the entire landscape of our awareness to pass through the worldly self to quiet depths where nothing is present and everything is present at the same time.

## Practices of Offering

There are many practices of offering. It can be like taking shelter from a storm in the safety of our house. But the house we are speaking of is the house inside of us, within the heart. People in all religions take shelter from life's difficulties. This is offering. We can find silence or peace as our shelter. Our hearts rest. We have shelter. Taking shelter is to take refuge. We can take refuge in our river of being, God. We can take refuge in everything that is good. When we take refuge, our hearts feel safe. In this safety the people or problems we are carrying in our hearts find another place. We have more of ourselves again.

Offering can be as simple as repeating the name of God or being simply thankful. Through the repetition our awareness softens. The world is not so intensely within us. Repetition like singing a mantra, God's name surrounds and enters deeply in the heart. Offering can be remembering to feel the Earth under the feet as a way of remembering to find our own ground. Nature is always offering itself and can be a reminder for us to do the same.

Our offering restores our innocence. In modern culture, we lose many parts of ourselves but perhaps most important we lose our innocence. Freeing the crowded heart naturally restores our innocence. This innocence we recognize in the children. And we recognize it when it is no longer there. At what age are we no longer innocent? In modern culture it is earlier and earlier.

> *As innocence leaves the faces of the young children, we can see the separation begin. A loss of innocence and gradually the soul, life's passion, God inside is also gone, buried within. Offering is a way of recovering our innocence.*

With innocence we are not so afraid and busy protecting ourselves. Our offering frees us of many real and imaginary fears. Life is passionate, bold, and vibrant. Life is new every day. In the restoration of our innocence, there is great trust in everything life presents us. We feel connected, trusting the day, each encounter no-matter what the appearance. Our offering frees us from fearing or doubting what comes to us. Innocence frees us from over reacting and making unnecessary barriers in life.

## *Offering and Receiving—a Necessary Balance*

Offering restores our ability to give. There is much said about giving. But most of us are severely limited in our giving. We do not know how. We may give our money or our time, but we do not know how to give ourselves. We do not know how to give because we do not how to offer and receive. We are told about the great saints who gave and gave. But no one talks about the process, his or her source of giving. No one explains the saints gave so much because they knew how to offer and to receive. They gave out of their inner abundance. This inner abundance calls us. Our inner abundance waits for us to be present and to receive.

Often people who can offer have difficulty receiving. Similarly people who receive life's abundance have difficulty offering. We see the poor giving freely and the rich seemingly holding onto every penny. This is the lack of balance between offering and receiving. Both are necessary. As important the offering is in all religions, it is equally important to receive. Life is offering and receiving God's love. This is joy's calling!

Our offering makes room to receive. One without the other is incomplete. The roots of our difficulties, our smaller self can seem stubborn and seeming immovable. We try cut them back by changing our behavior, thoughts, or feelings. In psychotherapy we try to examine their beginnings by remembering past dramas and childhood pains. Or we try visualizing our small self crushed or destroyed. In spirituality, we try to surrender to a higher power but without learning to receive our higher power, our small self persists. Often no matter what we try, we are unsuccessful. Our small self is the place inside of us that hungers for love, acceptance, trust, joy. It is the part of us that hungers to receive.

We are trapped in the anxiety and fear of our small self because we do not know how to receive.

> *Our energy, the self we know everyday, is trapped in mental worlds with no place to go, no relief at hand, no path out of the seemingly endless cycle of our thoughts and compulsive activity. Its as if life is squeezed into a small container. We think this container is normal and all there is. But through offering and receiving we discover there is a much greater container for our self. We are a river of self. And slowly we discover there is more then a river. We are an ocean of being.*

When we live separate from our river of life, we find ourselves constantly judgmental. What most of us see first in our selves and in others is what is wrong, what needs to be changed, what we do not like. It is difficult to see what is right, to enjoy the best of others and ourselves. We are focused on what we do not like and try to stay comfortable avoiding our dislikes as much as possible. We are challenged to enjoy the very best of life. We are challenged to receive the highest qualities of ourselves and each other.

Discovering real food, coming back into our own river, is learning how to receive. When we receive the highest qualities of life, this love enters the roots of our small self. Our fears begin to dry up, wither, and go away. The small self is neither so strong nor dominating. When we receive the very best of ourselves, our soul begins to take root in our awareness. As we identify with this new awareness, our identity begins to change. We begin to have an identity of what is right about ourselves and beautiful.

### Receiving Our Highest Quality

Receiving is more than thinking, more than acknowledging. It is something even more than accepting. Receiving is enjoying. Imagine living the highest qualities of our self, God, the brilliant love inside of us. Receiving is closing one's eyes and letting our awareness go as deeply inside as possible. Here we want to be like a sponge and absorb the pure lightness of being, the soft space, the depths within us.

> *After projecting our identity so frequently and intensely in the world, we want to receive the identity waiting for us inside. We also have an identity of simple awareness that is vast and pure. This is the home of our soul.*

This inner being is the love our smaller self misses. This is the joy, which heals our separateness, allowing the misplaced energy of our fears and anxiety to transform. We all have had experiences where we relaxed so much that we finally felt rested, felt ourselves. This relaxation may be after a weekend in the mountains or a vacation by the sea. We come home feeling ourselves again. We have had experiences of receiving a new friend, a new lover where nothing else exists but life's perfection, joy. The effects of these experiences, however, are usually short lived. We do not know how to stay with the experience. We do not know life as a path of receiving. Quickly we begin looking and finding what is wrong, what needs to change, what we dislike. To receive joy continuously in our lives requires us to have a life of offering everything we carry in our hearts then there is always room to receive. With practice, offering and receiving, real food and joy become as natural as life itself. As joy grows in our lives, the awareness of our soul takes root. For most people, their small self is securely rooted and memories of their soul, their wholeness, are few and fleeting.

Receiving takes great courage. We want to be open, vulnerable, humble, willing. In this openness it is very natural to have lots of feelings. We have tears of longing, sadness, laughter, tear for all kinds of feelings. The tears are from receiving, remembering our original innocence. Instead of being concerned with what others may think, we embrace our vulnerability, our feelings. Tears are the blood of the soul. As we get closer to our true self, tears come easily, healing, reconnecting us with ourselves. We have the humility to have our feelings. They are beautiful. We want to be willing to have our feelings, to let our tears come when and how they wish. True courage is the courage to be ourselves.

## Saying "Yes" Completely

We want to say "yes", completely "yes". Most people are afraid. With the decisions they make everyday, the experiences they are choosing, they are saying, "yes but", "yes maybe". If we really say, "yes" our small self may feel overwhelmed. If we really say "yes" all kinds of feelings may come. Exactly, these are the feelings, which bring us back to our self. To be overwhelmed, to let go, if necessary to drown, this is joy calling us. Of course we do not drown. It is only our fear, our resistance, which at times feels so large, and our hearts so small. Our inability to receive makes the decisions and choices we make into something difficult, something other then yes. We live a qualified yes because we are afraid to fully live "yes". It is joy that heals our daily world of "yes, but". Slowly, our life is only "yes". This is our soul unfolding in our hearts and in our lives. Imagine saying, "Yes" to our relationships. "Yes" to our work. "Yes" to our life and really feeling it!

To receive deeply is not something we do once. It is a way of life. To receive is to say, "yes" to our original innocence. Saying "yes" is receiving the very best of each moment. Instead of seeing and judging what is wrong. Joy calls us to receive the very best of what is present. Here is passion, peace, the lightness of being. As we learn to receive the very best in the moment, we begin to see and enjoy the best in difficult times as well as easy times. They are parts of the same river. It is a cultural habit to live judging, seeing what is wrong, what we do not like, and want to change. But this seeing, our judgments, only keeps us separate and unhappy. Joy calls us to receive the very best of our friends, partner, family, and our parents. In healing our relationship to important people in our life, the first step is in letting go of wanting them to change. The next and most important step is receiving the very best of them.

Most people stay in a struggle with their partner, their good friends because they are still struggling with their parents. The struggles are often from long ago but nevertheless in their thoughts and actions. We want our parents to change and love us as we want to be loved. Giving up this struggle means giving up our wish for our partner and parents to change. Joy calls us to receive them as they are. As we learn to receive the best of our parents and our partner, we become free of our struggle.

## *How do we receive the best of the other?*

Receiving the best of one another slowly changes our patterns. Receiving and enjoying the other is not a duty. Receiving is not something that happens when it is required or something we should be doing. Receiving begins in our being, being with the other and ourselves. Fear and separateness get smaller. Something else is growing. Receiving ourselves or someone else is not in what we do or how successful we are. Receiving is in the silence we share, the simple presence of life in us and with us. Receiving begins in the beauty of the moment. In the beauty of the moment, disappointments from the past and wishes for the future succumb to something greater. This is a practice when we are with our partner, parents, or church.

Even if we are physically separated from our love one, it is never too late to receive. In remembering the best of them, their smaller self, the separateness that affected us begins to become less. We begin to remember the greater, the unique presence of being and love that each person is in our life. Receiving the best of the other heals the hurts, the separateness in all relationships.

> *Joy, the seat of our wisdom tells us, we represent the very best of our parents who represent the very best of their parents. In truth, the very best of our parents and their parents and their parents and their parents for hundreds of generations is inside of each of us.*

We so easily focus on what we inherited that is wrong or challenging from our parents. We forget that we have the finest genes, the traits that have survived. We represent the heart of hearts, which has been selected again and again as the strongest, most whole, from all of our ancestors. We are literally the best of all previous generations. In addition to having tests for what weaknesses may be in our inherited genes imagine knowing the strength of our inheritance. Imagine coming into the awareness that we represent the very best of our parents, our grandparents, their grandparents and so on. Every generation did the best they could. We represent the best of them not only physically but in our whole being. Offering ourselves to our ancestors is to become available to the very best of them in us and with us. Receiving the best of life, our inner abundance is naturally overflowing in giving.

# *Our Nakedness, Our Vulnerability*

Our offering and receiving bring us increasingly closer to our essence, our heart of hearts. We are naked. Underneath the worries and concerns, desires and expectations that we offer, we are naked. Similarly in our receiving, life's intimacy is very naked. Joy is naked, pure, and true.

Life is less an uphill struggle and more a beautiful journey as we accept our nakedness.

Many of our problems are in fact not problems; they are simply our resistance to life's vulnerability, our nakedness. People struggle to change a situation instead of learning to enjoy the current season of their life. Many of our difficulties are just our fear of our own nakedness. We are naked. No matter how much we have, how busy and important we think we are, we are still naked. We are afraid to be vulnerable. We run from our nakedness. We do not want to feel how fragile life is. We just want to be comfortable. But of course, as long as we are afraid, we are never really comfortable. We need more and more possessions, activity, and security. We never have enough. We are afraid of simply being. Fear is the fuel that often keeps us going. But as long as we are running from our nakedness, we are apart from our joy, apart from ourselves. Making friends with our nakedness is to discover another fuel for living. Making friends with our nakedness is to heal our fear. Joy is the true fuel for life.

## *Making Friends With Our Nakedness*

Underneath most of our modern problems is fear. And underneath our fear is our nakedness. When we are at peace with being simply blood and bones, needs and desires, thoughts and feelings, we begin to find something else. We find our simple self. We are a soul. When we are not running from our nakedness, we feel life's presence. Instead of running on fear, trying to be comfortable, another life opens to us. Making friends with nakedness is to discover our greater being. In every challenge and opportunity is the landscape of our garden, the season of our life, our nakedness. Love is most intimate when we are naked. This is joy's realm. Real food is always found in life's naked moments. When we are holding hands with our child walking through town or running through green forests, we are naked in this moment. Nakedness leads to a heart of great wisdom.

> *We come into the world naked and alone and leave the world simply naked and alone. When our awareness accepts and makes peace with life's vulnerability, fear is not running our thoughts and feelings.*

When we have peace with our nakedness, emotional and spiritual doors open for new awareness. Making friends with our nakedness, life's opportunities become very different. Fear does not dampen life's natural enthusiasm. Our spirit is free to express itself. Our soft essence fills our hearts and spreads out into our life.

Our nakedness brings us to an understanding of everyone around us. Rich and poor, healthy and sick, angry or giving, we are all naked. Accepting our own nakedness, we react less and are closer with everyone. Nakedness is our common point no matter how different our ideas, lifestyles, or behavior. We are all vulnerable. When we are at peace with nakedness, we are at peace with others no matter in what circumstances they are living. Our common humanity is greater then our different mental worlds.

The opposite of our nakedness is our self-importance. Self-importance is really a cover for our fears. Self-importance hides in all our efforts to be comfortable, to be in control. Underneath our life of self-importance is a new life, a life of joy. When we begin a life of real food and nurture ourselves deeply, we have less need to feel and be seen as important. Real food, by definition, does not feed our self-importance but touches us in our nakedness, our hearts. When our hearts are full, our thoughts and words have less need to hold tightly our worldly identity. When our hearts are being fed, we realize our efforts of self-importance are really empty. We find new priorities. It is self-importance, which separates us. Understanding our profound nakedness, life's beautiful vulnerability, brings us back to our stream of being.

Similarly, nakedness is not self-sacrifice and denial. Some people go in the opposite direction instead of being full of self-importance; they deny and sacrifice themselves as their way to eventual joy. However, self-importance grows a life of self-importance and denial grows a life of denial. How can people think punishing themselves can lead to joy? How do they think denial and sacrifice is joy's calling? How did pain and joy get so confused?

Nakedness is not some discipline of renunciation. It is not the mind controlling the heart, our thoughts over ruling our feelings in some system of beliefs. Self-denial and sacrifice are just another form of self-importance. Simple nakedness is neither self-importance nor denial. We just are. When we have real food in our lives, we do not need to be important or to sacrifice and deny ourselves. We do not need to look for extra comforts or pain and difficulty. Life naturally gives us times of comfort and pain. Our acceptance of nakedness gives us joy's strength, joy's truth to embrace both. Acceptance of our simple nakedness gives us equanimity. In our nakedness we know ourselves. Joy is not something we make independently of life. Joy is life.

*Nakedness is our simple heart, open, and soft, vulnerable, sweet.*

From our nakedness, life naturally grows and matures into real fruit, true substance. Our relationships, activities, our passions bloom and return to the fertile soil of our being. We see, feel, and know who we are without pretense or defense. When problems emerge, the source of the problems can be seen. When there are choices to make, the options are clear. Nothing is hidden. Nakedness and simplicity live very close to one another.

Taking a few minutes everyday, sitting with our naked heart, gently holding our vulnerability, we are making friends with our nakedness. We rest inside. Our thoughts slow down. Our awareness is softer. When we are more inside ourselves, the energy behind our modern problems finds another place. Nakedness is the simple soil from which everything in our life grows. Nothing is hidden. Everything is revealed.

Our vulnerability is the richness of life itself. The depths of our emotions and experiences begin in the rich vulnerability of our hearts. If we are not vulnerable we are living but not really alive. Life and vulnerability, like love and nakedness, all come from the same inner garden. As we come to our simple being, we begin to understand God is closer to us then we are to ourselves. Joy is closer to us then we think. Nakedness keeps us near the well of being in our hearts.

# The Five Inner Steps

Our nakedness brings us to the true temple, our hearts, our inner being. Here the steps we take make God and the life of our soul real and practical. When we honor our nakedness, we are ready for the heart practice that brings us closer to our true self, God inside of us. Many people do not know what to do with their feelings of nakedness and cover them in staying busy. But instead of covering our openness and vulnerability there are inner steps into the heart that await us. These steps heal our separate self, the life we live apart from joy, from God.

Our separate self is our depression, anger, selfishness, boredom, loneliness, possessiveness, anxiety, and fears. Our small self cries out in many ways. It does not want to be ignored, pushed away, hidden, and punished. Our small self is already hurting enough. Our small self is expressing the fears that keep us separate from joy, our vast being. Our small self is not the enemy to defeat, to repress, deny, or to conquer at all costs. Our small self is the vulnerability of our heart crying for attention, respect, and care. We end our separation and begin again the path of feeling God's presence in our lives. We can analyse it, take it a part, discuss it, read about it, and express its thoughts and feelings. We can struggle with the behavior that comes from our small self. We can try to suppress our small self and hope it doesn't come again. Sooner or later, our small self must have joy, the joy that transforms our scattered, broken energy, which feels small, separate, and alone.

Real food is the true calling of psychology and religion. Our hearts and souls need the inner steps, the tools that strengthen us against the voices of doubt, the energies of fear. Our small self needs the real food, including inner steps, which the mystics in all religions and great teachers of psychology have found. These inner steps give the love that heals, give purpose, and life meaning. Psychology and religion need to come back to the basics. The doorway is not complicated. Love is not complicated. This doorway simply needs someone there to help us, support us.

Real food includes giving our selves the opportunity to take the inner steps of heartfulness, understanding, compassion, forgiveness, and wisdom. These are the inner steps for our resistance, our fear, and our separation. These are the inner steps for our remembering the life of our soul. Real food is giving our selves the gift to honor and practice our own wisdom. As we develop these qualities, joy is strengthened. Our small self finds more room, space for other parts of life. These steps give the small self, self-confidence. With confidence we can find the steps to return to our true river. These small steps remind us that we are more then the behavior and difficult feelings we have. As we grow in heartfulness, understanding, compassion, forgiveness, and wisdom, joy becomes as natural as breathing. These attitudes towards life are like muscles for the soul. When these muscles are left unused, life is difficult and daily life is full of conflict. As these soul muscles grow and strengthen, life flows easily through us and around us. Our being moves like a child in the world. Children naturally have these qualities but they are not developed and supported. Older people once again find themselves with these qualities, as they grow closer to their souls at the end of life. Children and older people naturally have a smile and grace of heartfulness, understanding, compassion, and forgiveness. They have their own wisdom. They have a beauty, a joy which most people miss. For most, intellect and personality have taken priority. Without use, the muscles of the soul tighten and shrink. The soul weakens, withdraws into the depths of our heart, and becomes unknown.

As remembering our heart becomes a normal part of our being, we are struggling less in the world and reside more softly within ourselves. With understanding we accept our way and the ways of others. We understand there are many paths for everyone to win, to be happy. Compassion deepens our relationship with those around us and lightens our own difficulties. As forgiveness grows within us, we regain our innocence. Like children, we find ourselves forgiving quickly and living more easily. Honoring our own truth, our wisdom gives us the courage to live our joy.

# *Heartfulness*

Heartfulness is awareness, a remembering of the presence of our hearts. It is to take a pause before quickly reacting. We take a breath instead of finding something to say or to do about a situation. Heartfulness calls us inside ourselves to listen, to be. Remembering our heart is a step of detachment from the event to be more present with our experience. We bring our heart into the moment. The activity around us, our first thoughts and feelings move a little into the background. We are remembering. In this moment everything is not so crowded inside. The situation is not so intense or overwhelming. Heartfulness is more then thinking, it is reaching inside. It is remembering the presence of our own being. This act of being with our heart gives our personality and everyone around us a little more space. Heartfulness gives our fear room to rest. Our fears let go to something greater.

Gently, self-confidence fills the space where fear and doubt routinely enter. Heartfulness is an act of self-love. Trust is affirmed. Our lives, no matter what the situation, suddenly have a little more room to be, to move, to change. Heartfulness is a path of living with our hearts present. It is more then a feeling. There is a spirit, an energy of heartfulness that comes from deep in our being, our soul.

> *Heartfulness gives the opportunity for something else, another part of us to be present. Our thoughts and feelings slow down. We soften. Bringing our heart into the moment allows for love to come into the situation.*

Heartfulness is a form of patience. We see more of our surrounding. The obstacles are like boulders in our river of joy. It is not so easy to

97

toss the boulders out of the water. It maybe easier to allow our joy to flow around the obstacles instead. Rocks and stones are natural to rivers as obstacles of all kinds are natural in the flow of life. Heartfulness reminds us to be more. We can flow around life's difficulties instead of battling them head on. We are remembering our hearts. Instead of impatiently reacting to each surprising event or challenge, we find first more of ourselves. The process of bringing our heart into the moment is to exercise a muscle of the soul. This is heartfulness. Once practiced it is easily remembered. Heartfulness strengthens our awareness. There is more to our being and to others. We are our river of joy.

As normal as it is to be mentally busy, critical, disappointed, angry, anxious, doubtful, or afraid, heartfulness reminds us of the beauty, the potential of the moment. A door is opened for the qualities of our heart to be present. Gentleness, truth, sincerity, emptiness, grace, nakedness, humility, generosity, abundance, joy, trust, simplicity, kindness, deep being, there are many aspects of our heart. Heartfulness is a path supporting us to be in our hearts in this moment. We are being the qualities of our heart. In modern culture there is little support for heartfulness. Most people experience these qualities by accident or occasionally. The energy of thinking and doing rules everyday life. Heartfulness is consciously making room in our life for the different qualities of our heart. We are making a space for the garden of our soul. Heartfulness is a practice of including our heart in everything that we do, in every conversation, every moment of being.

Heartfulness is a step to being available. We are becoming available for the many qualities of our heart. This availability is for others as well as ourselves. Heartfulness makes it possible for those around us to think less and be more, to do less and feel more of their heart's presence. Most people live in a pattern of quickly thinking, behaving, reacting, acting. Heartfulness makes for a new way, a way of being present. It softens the sharp edges of our concerns, needs, criticisms and judgments. With heartfulness, even life's most difficult times find more of a giving nature. Heartfulness is an important step in gently broadening and deepening our awareness. The instant we bring our heart into the moment, we find a new understanding. Later compassion and forgiveness come more easily to us as well. Heartfulness is to take a moment and bring more of our full being into our awareness. There is always time to react. We are bringing more of our heart, our truth, ourselves into the conversation. Heartfulness calms the situation down in everyone. It makes room in others and our selves for the potential of being present. Heartfulness takes courage because the energy of the moment is pushing, pulling, moving us out of our well of being. In modern culture there is strong pressure to do something. Heartfulness is remembering. We are. It is a large embrace for our selves and everyone else. With heartfulness we can look, hear, feel, and open more. Heartfulness opens doors. The ground we stand on becomes bigger. Our inner ground grows in strength and clarity. Remembering our heart is to open the garden for many qualities of love to come into every situation. Freshness, vitality, surrender, peace, brotherhood, sisterhood, faith, lightness; the qualities of the heart are without limit. Clarity, vulnerability, softness, easiness, love, knowing, wholeness, bliss; each quality of the heart is an embrace for our soul. When we remember heartfulness, we are remembering God. This is the life of our soul, to remember God many, many times each day.

# Understanding

Understanding begins with heartfulness. Remembering our heart, we let go of some of our certainty, our strong thoughts about what is, what should be and what must happen. We begin to open and feel more of the situation, the other person, and our self. With heartfulness, our thoughts and feelings relax a little. The qualities of our heart give us understanding beyond our thoughts. So often a situation remains confused, complex, unhealed because there is a lack of heartfulness. Without heartfulness there is little understanding. Everyone is in his or her own box of thinking and feeling. Heartfulness frees us. Understanding comes from bringing our heart into the moment.

> *Like heartfulness, understanding is more then a way of thinking, more then a feeling. Understanding has its own spirit. It comes from deep inside of us. Understanding is in the presence of our soul.*

It is true awareness. Understanding includes reflection, deep knowing, and simple being. Our awareness finds it own natural course. With heartfulness our feelings of anger, hurt, fear have some place to be. The presence of the heart receives every thought, every feeling. Slowly, understanding can come into the situation. Without the presence of our hearts, our feelings and thoughts are fighting to be heard. There is no understanding. Heartfulness gives the space for healing, being, renewal. Heartfulness gives space for the spirit of understanding to enter our awareness, to enter every part of our lives.

Understanding is to remember the bigger picture. The garden of life naturally has stones, trees, and flowers, soil where seemingly everything grows and a place where nothing grows no matter how hard we try. We can argue and struggle with the weeds, rocks, and bugs but they are all part of the garden. We can argue and struggle with ourselves and each other when things seem difficult, unproductive, when nothing is happening. But it is all part of life.

Heartfulness allows us to have the understanding of the bigger landscape of our being. When we sit in the larger picture, the entire garden and seasons of our life, the challenges we have are less threatening, more understandable. Heartfulness allows us to come to an understanding of our personal garden, the landscape we are living in. Certainly some changes are possible. But the earth, the soil of our life naturally grows when the conditions are right. Why do we argue with rocks, weeds, and bugs in life? Each has its own beauty and purpose.

Understanding is real food. Taking time for understanding, we can find joy in the landscape of our being. It is much more joyful to find understanding then to struggle with what life presents us. Our difficulties may be coming from lack of understanding. We are arguing with life instead of enjoying.

# *Compassion*

In our understanding of the garden and terrain of our life, we naturally find ourselves having compassion. As heartfulness opens to understanding, understanding brings us to compassion. Like heartfulness and understanding, compassion is more then a way of thinking, more then a certain feeling. Compassion has a spirit. It is a way of being which comes from depths of our heart that is the home of our soul. When we remember compassion, we find ourselves arguing less and being more with what life presents. We find ourselves resisting less and going further into every season life offers us. When we are not complaining about the weather and trying to always change the garden, we are available to enjoy what is being offered. We are deeper in the heart of each conversation, more present with every activity. We are more open, accepting, and compassionate with ourselves. We find ourselves deeper in the reservoir of joy. Instead of ignoring, reacting to, fighting or compromising with life's difficulties, we are in our garden in this season. We find compassion for every part of us and what we see in others. We each breathe and live with the same fears and desires. Life's garden in every season has it beauty and truth. There is no one to blame. We are innocent. Everyone is innocent. In these circumstances nature is taking its course. Compassion brings us back to our common humanity. There are no good guys or bad guys or rather in everyone there are a good guy and bad guy. Everyone is usually doing the best they can. Compassion keeps us in the river of our joy.

In truth, compassion makes the river a little larger. We include others.

*The practices of the mystics include giving thanks for the difficult people in our lives. We sit with the most challenging people in our daily meditations in compassion. Our heart, the seat of our joy grows and the other often feels it! Everyone and everything is a natural part of life's garden.*

Compassion is real food. Instead of feeling separate from someone, compassion brings us back together again. Instead of feeling how we are right and they are wrong, compassion brings us to our common humanity. Instead of wanting to win and the other to lose, compassion brings us back to our common wish for well being. When we take the time for the real food of compassion, joy has the opportunity to reenter any situation.

# *Forgiveness*

Forgiveness like compassion comes out of a soft heart. Forgiveness, which is merely thoughts about forgiveness, is not really forgiveness. Real forgiveness is more then a certain way of thinking, more then a feeling. There is a spirit of forgiveness, a clear light of forgiveness. It enters our awareness from deep inside of us. With compassion we can have true forgiveness. Many times we want to forgive but we are really telling ourselves that we want to forget and move on.

> *Real forgiveness includes the heartfulness to have understanding and the understanding to have compassion. Then the heart opens and softens in forgiveness.*

When we simply pass over events and try to forget in the name of forgiveness there is no real joy. But when we soften in heartfulness, understanding, compassion, true forgiveness is possible. And with true forgiveness there is a return of joy.

Life's challenges are often calling for us to give or in other words find forgiveness. We cannot really forgive the other unless we are also gentle and forgiving with ourselves. Forgiveness is a force of healing. It is reacting less and being more with the other. A practice of forgiveness towards the people we easily judge in our lives makes our river of joy grow much deeper, wider. These practices of heartfulness, understanding, compassion, forgiveness are the building blocks for a strong life of joy. They are the real food, the inner steps we can practice, that strengthen the muscles of our soul. And where does forgiveness come from? It comes from no less then the heart of God, the true heart inside of us. There is a spirit of forgiveness that flows naturally out of joy's stream.

# *Wisdom*

The fruit of heartfulness, understanding, compassion, and forgiveness is finding our own river of wisdom. The spirit of heartfulness, understanding, compassion, and forgiveness brings us the spirit of wisdom. Wisdom is different then what we learn from books or from others. This knowing is felt deeply in our bodies. It comes from life experience. This knowing is not something others can argue with or take away. It is firmly rooted in our awareness. While others may have faith or a belief, giving our selves real food, the practice of these inner steps, result in actual experience. We know our truth. We know joy, our vast being. We know love, God, from our own experience. This last step is to honor and receive our own knowing, our truth. Wisdom does not give us arrogance but exactly the opposite. We find our common humanity with others. The company president is no more special then the homeless person on the street. Our hearts are the same.

> *Wisdom is seeing beyond appearances to the substance of reality. Instead of putting life into categories, wisdom is putting life on the altar of the heart.*

Instead of our thoughts and feelings separating our self from others, wisdom is unifying, completing, being. Wisdom is often just common sense of knowing what is best. Wisdom trusts our own instincts, intuition, and creativity. Wisdom is knowledge of our own being. Wisdom grows with listening and practicing our truth, sometimes with, sometimes without support. Wisdom includes the wisdom of not knowing and the wisdom to be and not think too much. Wisdom lives well in joy's soaring wings.

Most people have joy almost by coincidence when it comes their way. But our heartfulness, understanding, compassion, forgiveness, and wisdom are the river of joy. They are life's river naturally flowing. Wisdom is the awareness that rises out of the river that carries us! When life is complicated, when everything is seemingly difficult, we are separate from our full awareness, our river. Before battling the challenges, real food reminds us, nourishes our hearts. Our river of being flows again. A path is found. There are no promises, no excuses, no problems, which call us to abandon ourselves, our river. The river is ourselves, our way, and always joy's path.

Many people wait for the big joys of life and find themselves living dry, apart from their wisdom, their hopes, and wishes. Joy calls us to live now, discovering the little moments, which keep us in life's beauty, gentleness, silence, and love. Our river flows naturally, curving, bending, bubbling, resting in our joy. Life does not have the big swings of being so low and later so high. Life is not so much difficulty and then so much ease. Life is not full of extremes, great drama, and complex story. Life is more balanced, even. When God is seen only outside of ourselves, we can quickly grow far away from God and our natural wisdom. God is remembered in our hearts through our inner steps. Here we are never so far from our river of great being.

# IV. Life For The Soul

# *Our Personal Story*

Our personal story is the plot of our life. The chapters come and go. The characters and activities change. The successes and disappointments, the high and low points we experience, are all part of our personal story. Normally, we are so busy with our current story that we have little perspective of anything else. We are so busy with everything we are doing, we forget about the many moments, the little flowers in the landscape around our story. In the midst of the plot of our story, we miss what else each day is offering. People can be so preoccupied with the script of their story that they do not see beyond, to the side, and the life within them. They do not see it is only script. Life is more then following a script. Life is more then the roles and various positions we assume. We are full of possibilities, potentiality. There is a big inner life to remember and explore. Joy enriches our awareness. When our awareness is rich with our own essence, we see our personal story differently. We feel it differently. We are much more then our personal story.

For most people, the large issues of family and work keep them occupied. The soft moments with friends, in nature, joy's many possible avenues stay in the background. They go by hardly noticed. The demands of the day, the thrust of our story are what are important. We are so involved in the plot and how it is going, we forget it is only a story. Easy or difficult, rewarding or full of struggle, it is still only our story. Life is always changing. Our story moves on. Are we a slave to our story? Are we so focused on the main characters and theme of today that we forget about life all around us and inside of us? How many opportunities do we take each day to stop and find little paths along our way to explore and enjoy?

If we were to remember the pressures and doubts we had a few years ago and how they eventually worked out, maybe we wouldn't take so seriously our story and how it is going today. Maybe we would notice something more then the current plot. Maybe we would enjoy the story more, including the little moments all around the plot. Maybe we would struggle less with getting to the next main event. Some people cannot wait to find a partner. Then they can't wait to have children. Then they can't wait till the children sleep through the night and enter school. Then they can't wait until the pre teenage years are over with. Others go without partner and family. They cannot wait to finish school and begin their career. Then they cannot wait for a promotion to buy their first house. Then they cannot wait for another promotion so they can find another house further away from work for some peace and quiet. Then we are looking forward to retiring. Meanwhile, we have never learned about living. Life is always in struggle and expectation of what must follow. They are so busy trying to control the plot of their story that they have little time, energy, or awareness of how to simply enjoy life.

## *We Are More then our Story*

When we stand back a little from the book of our life, we see the story is always moving but we are more or less the same. The plot is changing but we are not changing so much. Some chapters we have more money and others less. Some chapters are exciting with new relationships and others disappointing losing friends and family. In the midst of everything, our joys and fears, our simple being is more or less the same. What we are giving and receiving in life is not so different from one chapter to the next. Who we are, our awareness of life around us and ourselves remains more or less the same. Through the years, the story of our life changes but the main character we can still recognize.

It is I. Some paragraphs of some pages are more exciting, others less. We are anxious or grateful, fearful or joyful all depending where we are in the story. The plot continues as our lives curve around the stages of the growth of our family and career.

*What is important is not so much what stage our family or career maybe at, but the quality of our being, our joy in the midst of our story.*

Most people are actively involved with the details of their personal story. They think the next chapter will make a difference. We forget, unless we are making inner changes and discoveries, the main character stays more or less the same no matter what the plot line. We forget our personal story is just a story. We are more than this story. Our story today is the clothing we are currently wearing. One day parent, another day working, the costume we wear pulls upon certain parts of us to be active in the world. We can be always improving or changing the costume we are wearing. Or we can ask ourselves what we are bringing into our story? How much of our self is present? How much are we struggling and resisting or enjoying and receiving the story we are in the midst of? Two people can have more or less the same story going in their lives. They both may be businessmen going into the same office everyday. Maybe they are teachers attending the same school every morning. However, depending upon how much of their being is present, how open and soft are their hearts, the choices they make in the midst of their story, can be entirely different experiences.

The life of joy calls us to dive and leap into worlds of being, regardless of the current plot of our daily life. What we do, what we have, what we plan are less important then what we are experiencing and how much we are available to the presence of the moment! We often hear or know of two people who have the same illness but have entirely different experiences. This is because we are more then our personal story. While most people are grasping for the highs in life and fighting the lows, joy calls us to find peace in both the highs and lows. The waves of life are at times easy or crashing upon us, either way we want to enjoy the deep ocean. We want to feel the presence of life's beauty and simplicity no matter what the current plot. There is real food for us in every chapter of our lives. The story goes on but we want to enjoy real food including the people, many soft moments, the passions we discover. While others cannot wait until the next chapter and use all their energy to end one plot to begin another, joy calls us to find our inner resources wherever in our life story we may be.

> *Of course, it is easier to live joy in the gentle times. But when we find joy in the midst of life's pressures and disappointments, we begin the path of becoming free in our personal story. This is very beautiful.*

To become free in our personal story, we are not so attached to how the plot moves. Everyone has more freedom. As we find more trust in our own river of life, everyone around us feels the support to trust themselves more as well.

### *Becoming Free in our Story*

One person becoming free in their personal story is a great support for everyone around to live with less fear, less attachment, more trust in their path, their joy. To become free no matter what the circumstances of our personal story is the true life of joy. When we find our inner beauty and peace in the midst of life's challenges or conflicts, we are becoming free of our story controlling us. We discover once again, the Creator inside and around us. There are always possibilities. We are infinite potentiality. Instead of being preoccupied with getting to the next chapter in our lives, our reward is finding our ocean of being now. Enjoying the real food, the nourishment of the presence of friends and family gives us strength to let go and let the story unfold. Enjoying real food gives us the inner peace to let our story be instead of pressuring ourselves about what to do next. Ultimately the plot is not so important. Surely, it will change. But do we have joy or are we waiting for another chapter, only to find ourselves waiting again? Are we living in our inner river of joy or compromising with lots of excuses? Are we living in our hearts or are we desperately seeking the love we want in our story? So quickly the chapters pass and who are we? Have we become free or are we fearful of the story ending?

We know that our personal story has only one ending. We die and leave our story behind. We know the pressures we were so busy with five years ago, now we hardly remember what they were. But here we are again worrying about and struggling with new difficulties. Why are we so invested in controlling and managing our lives when we know someday we will only disrobe from the entire plot and leave our personal story behind? Why would we be so involved with each chapter if it is only giving us another chapter to be attached and struggle with? Why do we take our current chapter so seriously when we know the next chapter is coming? Change is always with us. When are we going to become free?

An easier life is not necessarily easier to learn to be free in. Joy found in the midst of great difficulty is joy found forever.

> *We have choices everyday, to wrestle with the current plot of our lives, or find the silence in the story. There are many golden silent moments each day which can be real food for a busy mind and hurting heart.*

Are we open to the moments of pure life that feed us no matter how easy or difficult, light or challenging our story maybe?

Most people think and feel as if they are alone in their story. There is an awareness, however, enjoyed in many cultures, that knows that everyone in our life is part of us.

Together we are sharing the same story, the same dream. Together we are awakening to the simple truth that there really is no story. We are each here being true to our current costume in life. We are together, simply being in this moment of eternity. Some people in our lives challenge us, some love us, some give, some take. We are all part of the same play, following a script. The script changes but the question is always how much of our being, our joy are we living? How much are we following our script out of habit, judging and reacting to those around us from our own patterns? How about surprising those who are not nice to us? How about helping those who are most difficult to be with? How about playing with our story? With joy, we can do the unexpected, be spontaneous. We can have fun with our story. Yes, we have fun with our story especially when everyone is so serious about the current plot. Life is more then our story! Life is joy!

Letting go of our personal story gives us the opportunity to become free of the push and pull, reacting day after day to the events around us. Our mystical nature waits for us as we discover the part of us that is greater then our story. We can hold our plot lightly, knowing it can change in any moment. As we identify more with the real food in our lives, we identify less with the highs and lows, successes and disappointments of the plot of our lives. Being more and doing less, we live in harmony, surrender, creating joy through the cycles of pleasure and pain filling the chapters of our book. We are living quietly inside. No need for big dramas or attracting lots of attention. Simplicity rules as we are committed to real food. Real nourishment is always found in simplicity. The complicated life keeps us separate, entangled in our personal story. Simplicity frees us from the current plot as we discover something more inside of us, the simplicity of the moment. There is the rich presence of one friend in one phone call or visit. Self-importance needs others to see us as important. Accepting our normal self with love and joy, we do not need to look important, act important, do things that seem important. We are. This is enough.

*Our personal story is just the stage, the background for a full inner life. The secret is as real food finds priority in our lives, our personal story changes. We are becoming aligned with our joy.*

Without us realizing, as we choose moments in life that nourish us, we begin letting go of the activities and habits that give us little. As we choose friends who enjoy life, we begin naturally seeing less those people who live in judgment and struggle.

## The Story Will Follow Our Joy

As our hearts discover the difference between being nourished and being busy, the contacts we make, the meetings we have, the plans we embrace, all become part of our greater being. Our personal story is changing. Those around us are changing. As joy takes priority, our story follows. Soon, the plot of our life is following the river of our own energy, our true feelings and desires. At first we have our story. As we have more heartfulness, understanding, compassion, forgiveness, and wisdom, we get to the story behind the story. Slowly we get to the real story that there is no story.

We are not living for someone else or how we imagine we should live. We are living for real food. Everyone in our lives begin to feel the difference. As we let go of the importance of controlling the outcome of the various chapters of our life, the plot changes. The characters change. Our activities change.

> One person listening and following their heart affects everyone else around them.

As joy becomes the foreground of our awareness, our personal story becomes more in the background. Life's plot, the details are not so important. Joy, lots of joy, the simple joys, have taken over. We are not so invested in how this chapter ends or how soon the next chapter comes. We are living in the present. We are in this sentence, this paragraph, on this page. We are in no hurry to get someplace other then where we are.

We have a life of equanimity. Our body and physical world is part of the soul. The part we can see and easily feel. And when the body and the world cease we are only a soul.

When we are not so attached to what we do and what others think, our energy is free. We explore another path. As the affairs of the world have less hold on us, energies in the heart and hearts of others are more available.

# *Letting Go of Our Pictures*

We routinely live the pictures we have in our mind instead of finding our passion, our essence and living who we really are. We live through the pictures we are carrying losing contact with ourselves. We live out a program instead of unfolding our soul in our lives. We have pictures of how life should be. With each picture is an understood script. What we think, feel, and how we behave is organized from these pictures and scripts. There is a plan, an agenda. Life is built around this plan whether it is really true for us or not. The pictures we carry tell us how our life should look and proceed. Our thoughts and feelings are busy with the agenda that fills our day, our dreams, and hopes for the future.

Each day can be busy with the pictures in our minds. We have an idea, a picture of what work, relationship, home should look like. Our life energy is busy giving life to these pictures. Our days are planned, almost scripted hour-by-hour, creating, maintaining, controlling our pictures. Little thought is given to if these pictures are really what are true for us. Do these pictures come from our heart, our true being, or are they simply pictures from our parents, the media or somewhere else in the culture? We normally give little thought to where our pictures come from or if they really express our joy. Life can become a picture album with family looking like we imagine it should be. House, work, daily activities, all can appear as we imagine. The picture book can be complete but what is happening inside everyone in the photos? Is there life, passion, real joy behind the smiles?

## *Our Agendas Limit Life's Possibilities*

Life is more than the pictures, scripts, and agendas that seemingly run our schedules. We are life! And life is much more then creating and managing the pictures we carry in our minds. Who knows where these pictures really come from? Who knows if these pictures are our destiny, or just our way of trying to have control in a large world? Our pictures are indeed a very small frame compared with all life's possibilities and potential. Being busy with what our life should look like can be an avoidance of our real passion, creativity, and truth. We think we are responsible for these pictures. We live being responsible for something that often is not real or worthy of so much of our life energy. Maintaining a picture of how we think our lives should be can be like making a river for our life to flow in. We can make a riverbed, find a source for water, plan the route, remove obstacles, enjoy a little, before finding more problems with not enough water and more and more obstacles to over come. Meanwhile there is already an entire stream within us ready for us to embrace and let flow easily, naturally to its destination. The first river is the one we try to make to fit the pictures of our lives. The second river is the natural stream of our soul unfolding.

> *Making life happen is very different then living life and letting our soul unfold. It is the difference between trying to force the pieces of a puzzle to fit the picture we want or letting the pieces come together one at a time, day by day.*

Are we willing to let go of our pictures and see what life naturally presents? Are we willing to let go of our ideas of what life should look like, and be with what is already with and inside of us? Are we willing to let life present its own picture albums live, spontaneously, without our own pictures limiting the experience?

Many of our pictures manifest suddenly. We are young and we meet someone. There is an excitement, a special energy. We quickly talk about our dreams and pictures. We project the excitement of our soul unfolding onto the other person and the pictures we want to create. Before we know it we are married busy making the pictures come true. Soon marriage, baby, school and vacation pictures all come. But long ago, the relationship itself was lacking truth. Couples can be more involved pleasing the other and making pictures, then being in their own river of joy. They jump into the perceived security of finding someone to make their pictures come true. They jumped into making a life for their pictures before they ever found what their life was really about. A life of little joy does not get suddenly happy finding someone to make pictures with. A life of little joy first must find real food that nurtures our passion and essence. A life unfolding our soul can unfold with another who lives his or her joy.

## *When Change Is Threatening*

The pictures we carry of how life should look can shape our identity, the ground from which we live. When these pictures change, our identity changes, our ground is shaken. Our pictures how our life should look fall apart. The picture does not match reality. This can be called ego death. We have projected our joy, security, self-confidence, well being into the pictures we try to maintain. Our egos struggle and sometimes crumble when our worldly identity changes. Many people are not prepared. It is difficult to accept change when we are holding a picture of a particular relationship or work as our identity. It is difficult to accept change when we are living separate from our inner river of joy. A new life can threaten seemingly our whole being when we are invested in how life should look. Many people suffer ego death. They are afraid to let go of their pictures of how life should be. The ego falls apart when significant relationships change or a job is taken away. The ego is threatened because we are so identified with our pictures of what our life should look like. The ego does not know what else to do. When our identity is based upon our pictures of what our daily world should look like, any change is threatening. We worry a lot. Or we search for some means to stay in control.

Of course, anyone who suffers a change in partnership or work has difficulty. But when we are living in our joy, we are not holding onto the pictures of our life so strongly for security. Our security is more inside, in our well of being. We trust more. We are more. Everyone reacts to difficult times with fear. But when we have real food in our lives, we react with less fear and more confidence. Our river is already finding a new course. Many people go through many ego deaths in life for example, going from one partner to the next. When life is projected outside ourselves, our partner is expected to try healing the separations we have from our own river of joy. With new partnership, our ego again grabs on and seeks new identity. The other person feels controlled and unloved for whom they are. Sooner or later, another ego death comes and we have to again let go of our pictures. Being so dependent, we are afraid of letting others have their freedom and be true to their joy.

Joy frees us from holding tightly to the pictures of what our lives must look like. Joy frees us from holding onto others as our ground, our stability in the world. It is natural, for example, to go through ego deaths as our bodies age and change. When we have our inner river of joy, letting go of our pictures, for example of being forever young and fit, are easier. We do not resist aging. Age has its own joys. People, whose identity is attached to the pictures they hold, suffer change and suffer a loss of purpose. Their lives were organized around making their pictures, for example a family and home. Who are they now? When these pictures are no longer true, where is life's meaning? What is our purpose? Are we here to make a pictures happen or are we here to unfold our souls?

With joy, we find our own ground inside. Changes in our bodies and the life around us are natural. The life of our soul is about remembering our inner resources. The map of our ego, making plans and pictures for the future can often be interrupted. Our soul is unfolding in the midst, around, and through the maps we are holding onto. This is our purpose to embrace our essence. Our personal story changes. The pictures we have grow old and we have to then let go. But our essence, our soul is ever present and growing in our lives. Life's meaning and purpose blossom as we come closer to home, closer to ourselves. We come home as we receive our soul blooming within us.

## Being All, Not Having All

Joy's adventure can also be full of pictures. People want success, partnership, children, and a spiritual life. They want everything. This feeling of wanting everything is a projection of the soul's reality where "everything" is already present. Everything is abundantly present. But often, we think this means we must "have" it all. So we struggle and persist in having all the worldly possessions, relationships, and spiritual life we want. We want all our pictures to be full and happy. This is a large projection of the abundance of the soul.

> *Life is much easier when we receive the abundance and incredible presence of our soul directly. Our ego wants everything. Our souls are everything. There is a big difference between having all and being all.*

Unfolding our soul in our lives does not flow with all our pictures. Many of our pictures are more about our egos being secure than real joy. Meanwhile, our souls are about being vulnerable, simple, and available for love. It is hard to be available for love if our minds are invested, controlling the pictures of having everything. Many people on joy's path also suffer ego death, which is the process of breaking down life's pictures to find what life really is. Life is naked. Each day is new. We are all profoundly naked. When our lives are about remembering our true nature, our essence then our soul can breathe, grow, and take root. Our soul cannot take root when much of our identity is rooted in fear, creating or trying to create pictures of what we imagine will make us feel better. Our soul unfolds in our availability to life, love's presence. Being busy with pictures is filling the frame of our life day after day instead of keeping it empty for what life presents. This is why we have a practice of offering, keeping our hearts free and clean for life itself. We let go of our inner pictures, untangling our personal story. We find our awareness softening, our natural innocence returning. We feel connected again. We are connected to life, to others and ourselves. Letting go of our personal story is the essence of the practice of offering.

When our partnership, work, activities, are an expression of our essence, we have no need for pictures. When we trust our children in being their own joy, the souls of each member of the family can be present. A family unfolding their souls is very different than family members living out life's pictures, life's expectations for the other. The feeling in the family is entirely different. The family members are friends, relaxed. There is nothing hidden. There is great joy. A family of souls, each in their well of being, feels free to create and express their joy. Each family member is supported to be big, abundant, joy full in his or her thinking and feelings. Each is supported in listening inside and to follow their own calling. There is nobody constantly reminding them to be practical, be responsible, not to want too much, not to expect too much, not to be too much. There is nobody telling them what to do, have, think, or feel. We are not here to judge how each other should live. Some parents can be so busy with pictures for everyone in the family, creating an agenda that there is little time left for life itself. Joy calls us to let each other find our own river of joy. Life without pictures allows deep trust in our own nature. As parents, through our own example, we teach our children to trust, live and be their joy. Then each member of the family can take responsibility, responding the best she or he can to life's needs and gifts.

Our pictures of how we think life should look are filters to what is already with us and within us. We can be so occupied with making our pictures of how we think life should look, that we know little about living. Our security is in maintaining pictures. New experiences, new people, new joys are limited. For many people their pictures are what guide them into their next chapter instead of listening and honoring what is in their hearts. Maybe a part of their life story should have changed or stopped long ago.

Living the ideas of how our lives should look instead of being in our joy, continue the struggle of our personal story. Why struggle trying to make our lives fit into our pictures when joy's stream is waiting for us?

Living our life holding onto some picture of how things should be keeps us from enjoying the spontaneity, the freedom, the joy we discover being present with what is around and in us now. In truth, life is never a picture. Our relationships, work, activities are always changing, renewing. Our pictures put a stop to real life.

> *Our pictures stop our fire from burning. They stop our water from renewing and our air from being. They stop the earth from giving new life. All the elements in life are limited or covered over by the pictures we put on top of life.*

It is tempting to follow the pictures of what we should do and how we should be that we receive from our parents. It seems easier to just live the pictures we have for our education, partner, work, home, vacations, the important details of life. Our parents pass on the pictures which often come from their parents and the parents of their parents. Countless generations before have had pictures of what life should and should not look like. Most of these pictures are full of good intentions. They can be beautiful. But are they our own wishes and dreams? Are they true for us? Or are they simply the unfulfilled pictures carried by those close to us? People who are not secure in their own ocean of being are often invested in how others should live. When we live separate from our own river of joy, we can be often judgmental and controlling of those around us. It may seem easier to try to live someone else wishes. But, of course this does not work. We must find our own destiny. No matter how much we may try to please others, they will not be happy. They must find their own river of joy as we must find ours.

## *A Leap Into the Unknown*

Letting go of our pictures, the photo album of how our lives should be, can seem to be a big leap into the unknown. But in truth it is making friends with our nakedness and vulnerability. We live through pictures because of our fear of life with out frames, life in its bold natural intensity. When we are present, trusting, living and being our joy, holding onto pictures is not so exciting. Slowly as we enjoy real food in our lives, we depend less upon this identity of maintaining the pictures we carry. Joy overcomes our fear of losing control. We are rooted in our selves, anchored in a life that is true for us. Our joy is giving to us moment to moment. We have stopped making photo albums and enjoy living instead.

As our soul unfolds, dreams and visions bring new pictures into our awareness. They are not necessarily a direction to go do something or to expect something to happen. They are just pictures which our mind makes sometimes instead of feeling. These pictures come from different parts of our psyche or soul. We can be with the pictures, enjoy them, and let them go. We do not need to hold on to them. If they are something for the future, they will come again. The pictures we receive in our minds and hearts do not make us special or important. They are just pictures. When we live in our joy, pictures of joy naturally come. They may be signs of events to happen or they may be just pictures to enjoy. As we learn to make our identity in our inner river, in life itself, we are more available for pictures or visions of all kinds. Being in our river, we are not dependent upon these pictures, we are supported by the depths of our river of joy inside.

To be in the perfection of the moment, to be with and let go of our disappointments, to enjoy and let go of our expectations, to let go and be in the beauty of this moment.... this is life without pictures.

# The Gifts of Emptiness

When we begin to see life as something much more then a series of pictures for our personal story to organize around, we discover our natural emptiness. Emptiness is our doorway to being more and doing less. Emptiness is joy's opportunity to come and stay in our lives.

In modern life, many people have seemingly everything. They live in large houses with family and plenty of income. They vacation in beautiful places. But happiness seems always to be fleeting, sometimes here and other times there. In their large house, they rarely feel fully at home. In their abundance is always some fear or anxiety of not having enough or losing what they have. They must stay on top of life's details, work hard, and remain focused on all the demands around them. Abundance and inner peace seem to be like oil and water. They do not mix. Underneath everything, they have a fear of emptiness. No matter how much they have around them, as long as this fear is present, life's satisfactions are few and far between. Joy never takes root and grows. The denial of emptiness keeps them separate from themselves and the abundance in their lives.

## Appreciating Winter

Usually we never find a partnership full of life or a work that is first of all fun. We are too busy running on fear's energy. We are filling ourselves up with everything but what we really want. An awareness and appreciation of emptiness is missing. We try to live a life of only spring and summer, forgetting winter is also important. Modern culture, in general, tries to exist as if only spring and summer exists. There is a need to be always producing, making new activity instead of trusting

128

the times when life is quiet and simple. Our need to always be productive makes real productivity impossible. Quality is sacrificed. People work more and more and feel as if they have less and less. They have less and less of themselves. In our denial of winter, we lose trust in our times of stillness, simple being. We lose trust in ourselves. The Earth, all of nature needs to rest in winter. Then Spring comes out of this quiet with new beginnings, fresh growth. We too need periods of deep rest, non-activity, emptiness. Winter is in an important season to have empty hands, to be still. Practicing letting go, holding onto nothing gives us the opportunity to be open, available, free.

Modern life is formed around being comfortable. Much of this need for comfort is our fear of emptiness. People want to be comfortable physically, emotionally, and spiritually all the time. In the need to be comfortable, we deny life's vulnerability. We are denying our nakedness. We are trying to escape the fact that our life too has seasons. We are trying to escape from life's natural emptiness.

We do not have heartfulness. And without heartfulness, there is little understanding the importance and beauty of having emptiness. Emptiness is time to remember our inner world.

> *Emptiness is a space inside where another part of us is present. Emptiness is a necessary part of life.*

Without emptiness, we spend our life energy running, pursuing, seeking. We struggle. We resist. We do everything we can to pass over or fill the empty place. But no matter how busy we are, how many possessions we have, how successful we become, emptiness is still present. Emptiness is a natural part of life.

> *Emptiness is the room where the soul can slowly open, breathe, and grow.*

When we have no time left empty in our lives, when we have no empty space inside of us, where is there room for our soul? How can we know God when we have no time or space for our soul? How can we enjoy the simple, pure presence of joy? Emptiness is not our enemy. The empty place in life is joy's opportunity, joy's potential friend.

But how do we find emptiness? How can we know emptiness separate from our fear and ceaseless activity? Usually we are busy with fear growing in our emptiness. We have a reoccurring feeling there is not enough. This feeling of not enough grows into life's problems, making life full of drama, a complicated story. Fear rules our awareness and prevents us from accepting life's empty moments. Fear separates us from the awareness there is enough. We are. Emptiness remains something to be afraid of, to fight, to fill up. Emptiness is not talked about in modern culture except as something to avoid, change, or not give our attention to.

Parents often try to possess and control their children. Employers over manage and rule their employees. Friends try to dictate what the other should or should not do. Underneath the expectations, attachments, and judgments we have, is emptiness. We often can be feeling how those around us should live instead of looking deep inside and seeing our own emptiness. Then we let ourselves and others be.

### Fear Covering Our Emptiness

The empty place is never far away. When we examine what most of our thoughts are about, we discover it is usually a subject we are worried about. Underneath this subject of concern, beneath our busy thoughts, we find fear. Underneath our fear is our empty place. For example, someone is always thinking about work. Is there enough clients, money? Is there enough? Underneath these thoughts there is fear. The fear is growing in their empty place inside. Their mind stays busy with problems with work and all the possibilities of what may or may not happen. Meanwhile, the fears underneath all these scenarios continue. Emptiness is waiting to be embraced.

Someone else may be thinking about his or her partner. How do I change the relationship? Will the relationship continue? They are worried, wondering, what will happen? Underneath their thoughts is fear. Fear is growing in their empty place. When they spend time, listen, and be with this empty place inside, fear of partnership changing grows less. As we embrace our empty place, we find more strength of being. Fear lets go into something greater inside of us.

Someone else may be preoccupied with his or her health or the health of a family member. Under the constant stream of thoughts is their fear. Underneath their fear is their empty place. When they make friends with their empty place, they are worried less. More of themselves is available for healing or being with the person who is not well. Being with the empty place inside frees us from the fear. More of our being is present and grows inside of us. Inside we are well.

*Emptiness makes room for joy's way to find space inside of us.*

The peace frees us from the fears that are growing into life's difficulties. Most people cling to a hope that something or someone will fill life's emptiness. They hope the coming success, new medicine or activity will make a difference. There must be a magic bullet, something to satisfy life's emptiness. We find little or no support to acknowledge and be with the empty places we find in life. We are told to have courage, do not give up, to fight. We must conquer, change our life. Change, however, more often then not just moves the emptiness around. Emptiness cannot be conquered, covered up, destroyed once and for all. It is a part of us, part of life.

*Courage is to be with emptiness. In life's emptiness we find there is something more. We are a soul.*

### *Emptiness is a doorway*

Some people confuse the gifts of emptiness with thinking they must be poor or live with very little. They think they have to give up everything to find inner peace. In truth they have to give up their fearful self. They do not understand whether they live in a large house or in a card board box on a street corner, emptiness is more about our attachment to our possessions then having many or no possessions. Emptiness is an understanding of the heart. It is not in how much or how little we have but in the realization that everything is temporary. Our possessions are a gift and not something that is really ours. Everything we have could be gone tomorrow. The wealthy have problems letting go and opening to their emptiness. The poor have difficulty feeling worthy of the gifts of peace and well being which come with emptiness. Rich or poor, emptiness is a space inside of us that either lives with fear and possessiveness or peace and expansiveness. Living simply keeps the gifts of emptiness nearby. Simplicity is a matter of the heart whether we have many or very few possessions.

When explored, emptiness is found actually not to be empty rather it is a presence inside of us. This presence is a vast, warm ocean of being. Sometimes light, sometimes dark, it simply is. As we befriend emptiness we discover it embraces us. No part of us is left untouched. There is no enemy to fight inside but simply a vast space to let go in. The space of emptiness invites our awareness to unload everything we are carrying, to relax, to experience being, to rest. When we relax and let go into the emptiness, our daily world becomes very different. We are not so anxious. We are less concerned with tomorrow. There is less room inside for fear and more place of trusting.

When we are available to life's emptiness, heartfulness takes the place of fear. This heartfulness grows. We find ourselves more understanding. We see how our daily life, our culture in its separation from emptiness, struggles, resists, and makes difficulty where it is not necessary.

We see our own struggle with emptiness and understand others more as well. So many of our problems are not what they seem to be. They are a problem in accepting emptiness.

*So many of life's challenges are not really challenges at all. They are a fearful energy making a temporary home in life's emptiness.*

As emptiness is accepted as a natural part of us, we understand the nature of life. Every activity, every relationship, every thought and feeling is also empty. Our daily world is temporary. Our daily world is ultimately empty. Underneath all our activity is this empty place. It is okay. It is in fact beautiful. Instead of always projecting our life energy outside ourselves into the world, we are being in our emptiness. Life is gentle. We are struggling less. We are reacting less to the demands of daily life. We have more of ourselves. We are with everything life presents. We do not take the anxious, fearful world so seriously. Underneath it all, there is emptiness. The life of our personality, our small self, our separations rule less. The experience of emptiness and our vast inner being is being received. In emptiness, our awareness finds shelter, safety, acceptance, and much more. In our emptiness we are finding the root of our pure joy. Emptiness gives clarity. Clarity gives us security.

*Emptiness brings us to our well of being.*

We understand our fear leads to insecurity, and difficulties. Fear naturally enters, when we live separate from our emptiness, the ocean of being within. In emptiness, our understanding expands, and from here, we find compassion, forgiveness and wisdom.

Our compassion grows in emptiness. We find compassion for others when they are caught in fear and struggle. We understand where this fear comes from and why the struggles grow so large. We know our own awareness can so quickly forget emptiness and find similar fear and difficulty. When we forget emptiness, we become anxious and grasping for something to fill us. We live in this aloneness, this separateness. Without accepting our own emptiness, fears take over and become rooted in a life full of drama and compromise. No wonder joy becomes so infrequent. Our compassion grows as we see how much of our own life has been wasted in the separateness. We still can be at times a victim to this awareness. We know better but everyday we begin again. The empty place inside, calls to be embraced.

> *Emptiness is something we want nearby all the time to keep us in true perspective, in compassion.*

Emptiness gives us an unlimited source of forgiveness. We forgive the thoughts and activities that come from a denial of our empty nature. We forget. We have forgotten. Emptiness is reawakening us to our true essence. We forgive everything else, everyone. Who are we to judge when so much of ourselves has lived, traveling separate from the empty seas inside? We have spent so much of our life energy in running from emptiness. How many hours adding up to years is spent in worry, self-doubt, seeking security where there is none. We have searched and struggled so much in the world when the answers we sought were inside of us. In our emptiness we find our vast being waiting to give and complete us as nothing in the world can. From our own journey returning to emptiness, we naturally forgive the lack of awareness in others.

We receive life's joy when we are not preoccupied with anxious thoughts and fears. As we make friends with emptiness, we are not in struggle to fill life up or change it. When emptiness is accepted as part of life, we freely receive what is given.

> *As most people are busy trying to fill the empty places in their hearts, their homes, their day, we find what is already present. When empti-*

*ness is not ruled by one's fear, a vast and beautiful space is discovered.*
*This empty space in life is the playground for the path of joy.*

When emptiness is accepted and becomes our friend to listen to, to
appreciate, to make room for, the inner life changes. Our daily world
changes. Emptiness is the bearer of gifts. Life's joy goes hand in hand
with great emptiness! Emptiness is the door to many new beginnings.
Life's fullness has a place to be received. Without emptiness, the fullness of life is pushed away, diminished, or somehow made less. Instead
of enjoying everything given, worries grow and spread about what is to
happen next or some other distraction. Worries are like weeds that take
over when the ground of emptiness is not recognized and cared for.

## In Times of Difficulty

Everyone finds at times reoccurring difficulty that seems beyond help
by the experts. We find parts of life beyond help from our own physical
and mental efforts. These are the times of winter. Emptiness calls.
Spring, a new beginning will come. But first let us curl up inside next
to the warm heart of emptiness. Our reoccurring difficulties push and
pull us to explore our soul's domain. Underneath the hard everyday life
is a soft center. The story of our difficulty is not the whole story.
Underneath the drama is the territory of the soul. Sometimes nothing
in this world is meant to occupy the empty place. Now is our time to
be, to feel the touches of God's lightness. The angels are very close to
us in our times of vulnerability, emptiness. Our difficulty calls us to let
go of our fears, our attempts to control, and to make new awareness of
life's empty place. Emptiness removes our fear of death. This fear is at
the root of many difficulties, especially our difficulties of letting go, letting be, and letting the new come. Emptiness gives us the experience of
who we are beyond death. We can let go. We are.

We are not here to make drama, for drama to run our life. The empty
place is the home of simple awareness. Life's waves come crushing

down on the surface of things but joy's river brings us through life's everyday currents. Our difficulties can be reminders of the deep ocean of being calling us. This is how joy's path can radiate peace in the midst of life's turmoil. We see the big waves, which have caught everyone in the moment. But our awareness is in the ocean where the waves are quite small and inconsequential. When emptiness is embraced, the difficulties of the world find fewer places to grasp and hold onto.

Emptiness is our way of being in the present. In the vast well of emptiness is where the richness of friendship, love, nature's beauty, and God's peace is received. Emptiness is perfect medicine for any ailment. With emptiness, the mind and body are not clinging, pulling one another in opposite directions. Fear is not sinking its roots further inside the nervous or immune system. Healing can take place.

> When emptiness is king and queen of one's life, there is no ruler but truth itself. No dogma, doctrine, fear, or controlling force is governing our own true golden nature. When we bow down each day to the emptiness in all things, each encounter, every moment, the perfect presence is experienced.

As we explore emptiness, we are exploring the frontier of our soul. This is our spiritual body, the body of eternity inside of us. Each meditation is a further exploration. When the time comes to let go of our physical and mental bodies, we are not so surprised. We find our awareness in our spiritual body, this vast space. As our being expands without the physical world limiting us, it will be natural. We will recognize and remember our path of eternity. The mystics and saints know their spiritual body. They do not resist emptiness. They live in their vast space of being. This is why people can feel their presence from long distances away. The great teachers live in their spiritual body while most of us have only brief experiences of our vast being.

In our emptiness we can rest in our awareness. We are free of thought, feeling. We are free. We let go in our vast being. We remember how much peace, safety, gentleness, is at our core. We soften into the openness. When thoughts float by we let them continue floating. They are not important. We are breathing into the depths of our awareness. Every venture inside is new, warm, welcoming, embracing, protecting, joyful, or light.

## *Being Free in Emptiness*

Our habits, addictions, compulsive patterns of thinking and behavior all have roots in emptiness. Knowing emptiness, we see where our thoughts begin. We see where our habits and patterns grow from. Embracing emptiness, we can let these thoughts and patterns go. Our personality in its true nature is empty. The thoughts and behavior we would like to leave behind may or may not change. But we know, these thoughts and behavior, no matter how attached the roots maybe, are ultimately empty. They have no power. We practice observing how a thought builds and then another comes and connects to the first. Then more thoughts join. We practice watching our personality slowly developing, connecting thoughts and feelings, coming into our worldly identity.

> *From this emptiness, one thought at a time, all our opinions, inner structures, interpretations, judgments, the weight of our personality, come. How we live, how we are in relationships, everything we are in the world comes out of emptiness. From emptiness, we see how we give meaning to our daily world and how we can simply be, free in emptiness.*

Emptiness frees all our attachment to thoughts, feelings, relationships, all our activities. When we are free we can truly enjoy. We are free to say "yes" or "no", to come or to go, to dive into the depths of life or sit quietly in the silence. Emptiness gives the life of joy choices, space, heart, unlimited possibilities and potentiality. Emptiness is the home of our awareness before we divided life into thoughts and feelings, before we separate I from them. Emptiness is who we are before separation and afterwards, where we come back to our true nature. Every time we let go of the world we are carrying, we can rest again in simple emptiness. From this awareness of nothing but space, we see ourselves and daily life differently. "What is the self?" "Who am I?" These questions find easy, gentle resolution. "I am empty and full, nothing and everything. I am this endless space carried in eternity."

This space in which our awareness finds home, gives us another outlook on the home in the daily world in which we can be so preoccupied with. Our everyday activities are not so consuming in who wins, who loses, who is right and who is wrong. Our ideas and mental worlds are seen differently. Every time we live in my true body, our spiritual body, we take my physical, mental, and emotional self less seriously. We hold onto our self and everyone else a little less tightly. We have more space inside for joy. Joy is the open hands, soft heart, spacious awareness that comes from our experience of emptiness. Everything, everyone, comes and returns to emptiness. Everything we carry, other then emptiness, is a weight keeping us from climbing down the ladder of Paradise inside of us.

# *Our Ground of Being*

In truth, emptiness is not empty. It is our ground of being. Instead of looking outside of ourselves for our security and comforts, we find more and more self and true being inside. Embracing our emptiness is to open a room within ourselves, which is vast, warm, and full of presence. Our presence. One step inside into emptiness can lead us to worlds of being. This is God inside of us.

*God is our true ground of being.*

Our ground is where we stand. From the ground we stand upon, we build our identity, our home, work, and relationships in the world. For most people their ground is literally their house, their place of work and where they spend most of their time. When home, work, or daily life changes, their ground is shifting. The ground under their identity, their foundation seems to be moving. Their ground is never very secure because life is full of changes. Fear is always near by. They are busy trying to control things, to stay on top of things, so their ground is firm and stable. They seek titles, large bank accounts, status, anything that will give them security. Others become victims of addictions, compulsive behavior. They feel themselves most, their ground, when they are in difficulty, ill, or suffering. They suffer again and again because this is the ground of being which is familiar. The ground, which they at least know. However, there is no activity, difficulty, or identity in the world that replaces the joy of knowing our ground of being. True ground is not in what we have, what we do, or what we think. Our security is in our ground of being. Real food brings us to our ground of being. Our ground of being is what our awareness stands upon. Our ground is infinitely solid and whole. Everyday, true joy calls us to begin again, to begin fresh. Our ground of being is found in our honesty, our truth, our well of being. From our ground of being we can make wise choices.

Whenever or wherever life becomes complicated we have grown far from our ground of being. We are separate from our creative source. We see ourselves as a victim or are busy blaming others or the situation for our troubles. As we find our own ground again, we see our difficulties and others differently. Our ground of being gives us back our independence and wholeness. Some people wake up one day to find themselves in the wrong work, wrong relationship, living in the work city. They are disconnected from their true ground, their ground of being. They try new work, new relationships, move and maybe move again. The same problems follow them. They are separate from themselves, their ground. Without our own ground, a true life is impossible.

### What Is Bringing Us Back to Our Ground?

Life's difficulty and pain have meaning in as much as they bring us back to ground, to the beginning where joy can start again. Life's challenges serve to clip our wings, at least for the moment, and bring us back to Earth, our Earth inside. Here we begin again with heartfulness, with the inner steps, to find joy. Many times in our life we are brought back to Earth, our ground to begin again. The winters of our lives serve to bring us to new spring and new summer. Eventually we let go again into another Fall. When we are pulled to the ground by life's circumstances with nowhere to go, no one to turn to, we are being taken underneath the details of our personal story to the ground of our hearts.

Friendships, work, home, everything is changing as we are letting go into Fall. There are times when everything is still, quiet, and empty as the night of winter. And there are times when new love, new creativity is bubbling from inside like the blossoms of early spring.

*In each season we have our ground of being. We are open and available for the beauty and mystery of this season.*

With our ground of being, we are not trying to control and manage the weather, the shifting circumstances of our daily life. Every season is special, full of mysterious, wonderful presence. In every season we are vulnerable yet strong in our ground of being. Our ground of being supports us. Each season has its unique beauty. Living in the heart of each season, we are close to the eternity that is the ground of being, the quiet in the midst of life's movement, and perfect stillness in the action of life around us. Eternity grows in meaning as we stand in our ground of being and let life's seasons flow through us and around us.

Our security does not have to be so attached to our places of living, our health, relationships and work. Our ground is in our joy, our well of being. When we remember our ground of being, we are remembering our vast self, our inner resources, our truth. Our ground of being is this pure place inside, our innocence. Discovering our ground of being is the next frontier in consciousness.

Most people do not feel their ground of being. Their awareness goes to the largest demand or the loudest noise in the moment. They are projecting their identity outside. Life is their activity in their daily world. Even God is thought as someone or some force outside of one's self. When we are projecting our life energy constantly into our activities, relationships, and work we are more and more separate from our selves. When God is imagined only outside of ourselves, it is no surprise we feel separated from God. This projection of our life energy demands great effort as we try to create, maintain, and control the events of our lives. The task is overwhelming. Many people are depressed, tired, feeling separate from others and themselves. When we lose our ground, we lose our energy, sense of self, our life energy, and purpose. On joy's path, instead of projecting our life energy outside, we find more energy inside. Instead of projecting our identity constantly out into the world into our daily successes and disappointments, we are finding more of ourselves inside, our passion, our creativity. Our separation ends as we find our ground of being. This is God, life, the pure presence within us. Here we are not alone or lost. We have our own ground. There are many words for this experience. As intellectuals debate and argue ideas of true self, joy's calling is about going inside ourselves, our nakedness, our hearts and remembering our ground of being. Here we know our selves. The feet of our awareness are on solid ground inside of us.

The steps to our ground of being are one at a time. They are the inner steps, our heartfulness, understanding, compassion, forgiveness, and wisdom. They are the steps becoming free in our personal story. As we let go of the pictures we are attached to, how our lives should look, we are remembering our ground of being. The ground of our awareness frees us. With fewer thoughts, feelings and struggles occupying our awareness, we find our ground of being growing our inner garden. We know another way. Instead of attaching our identity solely to relationships, work, every day activities, we embrace emptiness, our groundless ground of immense being. We identify each day with simple being, simple joy. Our ground of being is immediate, secure, vast, and powerful.

### Security Inside

The usual worldly identity we have can change. Our ground of being is the same. We stand in our own certainty. We are remembering the friendly space of emptiness. The place inside is relaxed. It easily lets go into our own full being. Inside we are secure. Here lays our ground of being. On good days or bad days, it is the same. The ground of being is always. Normally with our worldly self, life is busy with no place for our awareness to truly rest, to be home. Now we are aware of our inner ground. With emptiness, we have found the ground where we are at home. There is no activity inside. No demands, nothing to do, we can simply be. In our emptiness, we discover over and over again this quality of being, an awareness of carrying no thought, no weight, no concern. Our awareness takes root and identifies with our unlimited ground of being. Our vulnerability and nakedness takes shelter in our ground of being. Our ground of being is clear, present. It is the size of the Earth itself. For some the experience is like being one mile inside the Earth. For others, it is being in the Earth and beyond, their ground of being is the size of the universe, all the planets and the stars. Our ground of being is without border or limit. When our awareness lets go into our ground of being it is like being held, protected, feeling completely received or accepted. On this ground we feel sure-footed. We can take refuge in our simple ground of being. This refuge is in joy, the ground of our being.

From the simplicity, clarity, truth of our ground of being we see our relationships, activities, worldly self, differently. We are not seeking or holding on so tightly to others or our activities for security. Our friends, family, work, all our activities can come and go. As our awareness rests in our ground of being, we are less dependent upon others for our happiness. We have our joy. We have our simple ground inside. As we identify more with our own inner ground, we are not seeking to control or take possession of objects, people, work in the world. We can let go and be more in all circumstances. We are less threatened by events around us.

> *Inside there is no waiting, no worry, we are with our true treasure, our golden unlimited being. We are living in the world but more and more our awareness is in life's true wealth, God's presence in life itself.*

Our ground of being is our inner security that the great saints and mystics found and lived from. God is no longer only a belief but a very real experience. It is a mountain of truth, our truth of being. Our ground of being is the most fertile soil. In our ground of being we find our highest quality. Our peace, trust, love, and great being are all abundant. This is God's uniqueness inside of us. Here our creativity is connected to our core being. We can build mansions in this world or find mansions of being in Divine realms. When our thoughts and feelings are not so entangled in our daily life, when we have our simple ground, we are available to touch and be touched by our Divine essence, the Divine in many worlds. What we find in each other, nature, and our selves all changes. Many sources of joy become available when we are available. Our openness, intuition, creativity, our heart's capacity, have no limits when we live in our true ground. The miracles performed by sages of all religions begin from this ground. They are natural. This ground is pure awareness and from it anything, any act of love is possible. There are no limits to love's potentiality when it is grounded in truth.

Many times, people create small and large miracles when they say to themselves, "This is the truth". In this moment they see and know truth. There is no doubt. The truth manifests. This clarity and certainty comes from their ground of being. As we let go our fears, awareness becomes one with our ground of being, we understand. We know. We are.

# The Unfolding

After ten, twenty, fifty years of compromise and struggle, how do we begin again? How do we find our true ground? How do we consciously unfold our souls in our lives? Most people think right away about making big changes in their work or relationships. But after making the big changes in life, we are still more or less the same person. Our hearts have the same fears and desires; only we begin projecting these fears and desires into new places, onto new people. We can make big changes in our lives but often our hearts are not ready. We find large fears instead. The soul unfolds slowly, gently. Innocence and life's beauty grow again but in their own time. The heart recovers naturally as we find our true ground.

## The Dark Night of the Soul

Many of us are living the dark night of our soul and we do not even know it. Life has pulled us out of our river of joy a long time ago. We work hard for our identity, our place in the world. We care for it and defend it. An ocean of simple being is a distant horizon. The little light and joy we have, we think is normal. We have little idea of trusting our inner river, our feelings, our own energy. The idea that life naturally brings new opportunity, work, friends, meaningful activity is foreign. We are alone. The separation is so great we do not even believe we have a soul. This darkness is multiplied in times when life falls apart with loss of family, health, community, or work. We may not even know why we feel the darkness we do.

We cannot find our passion. Our lives in the world are full of difficulty. Or when we go inside ourselves, we feel little or nothing. Some-

145

where in our hearts, our soul, life's sea of joy has dried up. We are in a desert. This is our time of distance, being apart from others, ourselves, and seemingly everything good.

This is the time to practice conscious patience. Heartfulness is the first step in not judging ourselves, our darkness, by escalating what we are experiencing with more fear. Heartfulness gives us permission to explore this period in our lives feeling so separate from our own light. Then slowly we begin to hear joy's calling. One small joy at a time and the light slowly comes again. This is our time to begin finding real food. To find a moment of peace in our dark night is a great beginning. Slowly one moment builds to two and then another. To sit inside our own darkness, slowly there is less fear and more simple presence. Even if there is only darkness, we can listen to it, simply be with it. We begin to welcome the seemingly endless darkness. The rocks do move when we let go of trying. Something greater is with us, in us.

The dark night of the soul is an important period in finding our inner road map to the true life of our soul. Sometimes we have been following the path of others for our entire life, when we decide to find our own way. In the beginning we may find only darkness. This is part of the process toward finding our inner map, our own way again. Sometimes we try to live in both worlds, one life for others and one life being true to ourselves. Suddenly we find we can no longer be two people. We can no longer feel what is real and what isn't. We feel disconnected to everyone and everything. There is only darkness. As we grow older and lose some of our health, a partner, or work, we do not know what to do. We do not know our inner river, because we think our joy is dependant upon what we have and can do. Our loss brings us back to ourselves, the simple joys, and slowly we find joy's river again which is separate from what we do, have, and normally think.

We can be fixed in our excuses for not finding real food. We are sold on our beliefs that life's darkness is always with us. We may cite the problems in life and the violence in the news as proof. We do not acknowledge the vast majority of people quietly enjoying life's beauty and gifts. We live discussing how bad things are both personally and around the world. We are caught in a joyless life, projecting our current darkness into our view of the world that sees darkness permanent and true. There is little or no love right now in our lives. Or if we have love, we are keeping it within limits. We are busy looking for the shadow that is also present. We make darkness a fact, which means we limit love's potential. Joy's absence can make darkness very real. Keeping dark feelings near keeps joy's presence under control. Looking for the darkness, our shadow can keep love's vulnerability, love's wonder at a distance. Our attachment to having darkness can weaken or deny love's vastness, our peak moments and potentiality. Expecting life to have always darkness can be an excuse not to open our hearts to life's abundant grace. It takes great courage to open, experience and express our joy. Our beliefs about suffering can be excuses to not receive. Living in life's shadows is always sure to find fear and anger somewhere. When looked for, fear and anger can always be found. Similarly living life's simple peace can always find joy and beauty even in the midst of difficult times. Which do we want, fear's presence or the gifts of joy? What is serving our self-importance and intellectual identity and what brings us to life's gifts and true being?

Living joy is not to deny difficulty or our fear and anger's presence. However, living joy is not to make our fears and anger more important then they really are. Joy gives us our heart's balance, our heart's trust. We know when it is right to be fearful or angry. We know when it is right to let go and find life's simple beauty. The heart has its own wisdom, course and time for healing. It does not need formulas, techniques, or to be told what to feel. The heart's natural knowing comes from living joy's path. The darkness and shadow maybe nearby but does not mean that it is worthy of our awareness. Yet, sometimes it is important to see and understand the fear or anger that we are experiencing. Exploring life's darkness and shadow may be part of our healing. Darkness is dramatic and full of energy but it does not lead to finding life again, the simple joys. Being watchful of life's darkness can divide our attention. The world is dark enough with the daily news and fearful energy we are exposed to. Finding our joy and serving others offers much more to the world and ourselves then our ceaseless complaining about the news or life's negative events. Living in life's shadows limits the light we open to and receive. There is no shadow in the cloudless sky. The unclouded mind is the same.

> *There is no shadow in the experience of eternity. We just are. Darkness has no importance as we remember our innocence.*

The first step is in recognizing where we find real food in our lives. Real food may be when we are in nature, enjoying a certain activity. Real food may be the joy of no activity, in the time we make for simply being. Real food is receiving the pure presence of our children or a special friend. Real food is how God touches and reawakens our soul. It may be listening to classical music or the sounds of the wind or ocean. Real food softens our hearts and brings us to our ground of being.

Real food may be our experience with a particular teacher or teaching. Sometimes we are so hungry for the real food that we think this teacher and only this teaching is the truth. We find ourselves critical of all other paths. We are sure that we are enjoying the only real food. Our egos naturally think our way is the best and the only way. When our soul is touched, it feels so wonderfully real and true, we want everyone to know about it. We may spend a lot of time and energy trying to convince others of our right course. It is normal to become attached to the real food wherever we have found it. Our soul has been starving for true nourishment. In the beginning, we make our source of nourishment the center of our lives and may think everyone else should as well.

> *Everyone in their own time and way finds their own path to God. What touches the soul for one may do little for another. We have so many judgments and defenses to joy; it is surprising that we find a path at all.*

For some, finding real food is not so easy. They have been disappointed so often or so much, that it isn't clear how to find a true source of joy. The process for them may be first remembering the last time they found joy. As they remember the sources they have found at various times in their lives, they can begin looking again for similar sources. The soul, no matter how buried or hidden inside, leads us, guides us. The soul in each of us knows what is true nourishment and what is not.

During this period of conscious nourishment, layers of fear are slowly dissolving as joy is finding its home in our hearts and our lives. The life of the soul attracts the ideas, people, and opportunities that support its unfolding. Joy is reminding us that life is not a struggle, not something to accomplish and master. Our soul is our true nature. It is our simple awareness during the day and in our exploration at night. We may have dreams of flying, breathing under water, walking through walls, or being visited by friends or loved ones who have passed to the other side. We may have experiences of true connection with a teacher, old friends, or a stranger we just met yet somehow seem to know for years. There are moments, days, weeks where everything is going perfectly right. The right meetings, right activities, right responses, life is unfolding just as if everything and everyone has purpose and is on course. New security, new identity is being found closer to home, within our selves. As our source of real food is found and enjoyed, more sources begin appearing. We begin to recognize the qualities of this food elsewhere in our life. Slowly we begin choosing this joy, love, peacefulness in our relationships and activities. Our souls are unfolding and taking root within us.

### Challenges, Distractions, Resistance

Soon we find ourselves in a new period of life. We are saying, "yes" to our souls. We are saying, "yes" to life and letting go of the temptations to compromise and procrastinate feeling our joy. In the midst of this "yes" to life, however, frequently we find ourselves distracted and acting as if our soul doesn't exist. One minute we can be deeply enjoying real food and the next minute we can be reacting to events as if our peace and inner knowing never happened. This can be challenging. We can find ourselves in crises of identity. Our hearts are yearning for "yes" but we are still living in our old world of struggle, compromise, the world of being practical and cautious. How do we keep our hearts open after years of being more closed then available? How do we remember to be present? How can we say, "yes" to ourselves in such a non-joyful and fearful world? Our old friends, activities, and old patterns of relationships challenge our new path. The mind can find so many obstacles, so many "what ifs" to discourage our way. There are so many distractions. A true life full of heart is seemingly so far away. How can we expect to find the heart in the world, when we feel so little love of our own?

Like a small bird, our soul needs our shelter, care, and devotion. We find ourselves in great swings of emotion. One moment we are flying on mountain peaks and a little while later we are at the bottom of the pile, with the world's problems on top of us. The mood swings are the rebirthing pains of our soul. One day, everything is flowing. Life really is a river we can trust. The next day, nothing works, no one is there, and life is barren again. This period of remembering, renewal is natural. Slowly our souls are unfolding. We go back and forth, trusting and doubting, hoping and fearing. What is real? Who am I? Where am I going? What am I doing? The ups and downs, the highs of our joys and the lows of our disappointments make life like a roller coaster. But the soul is always greater. Our personalities and all our questions lessen, as the soul reemerges, step by step, expanding in our hearts. Our joy strengthens as we find true security in our own passion and river of being. Something greater than our own efforts is helping.

*It is important to remember that a part of us is already liberated.*

It may take some time for our personality and our daily life to mirror the completeness of our soul. But our soul is already the perfect presence of real peace. Our awareness does not often recognize it but there is an absolute reality of everything being present.

Meanwhile, it is important also to make room in our lives for our resistance. If unfolding the soul were so easy more and more people would be doing it. Living joy in a world that has lost its innocence is going to find again and again obstacles. The most difficult obstacles come from inside of us. Our struggles are not wrong, bad, something to get rid of. They are just the patterns we have that keep us separate from being present. In the moment of our lows, we can remember to breathe deeply and feel the presence of our hearts. We practice heartfulness. We bring our thoughts again and again to the present. We practice letting go of future worries and feel our hearts in this moment. We again have understanding. Our doubts give way to the beauty of this moment. Compassion for ourselves comes slowly. The friction and discomfort of our new life is to be expected. Our soul is finding room inside of us and in the world. Forgiveness comes more easily as we live heartfully in the present moment. We have been taught that life's answers and security were outside of us, sometime in the future. Security now in this moment is to discover joy's river growing inside of us. It takes time to feel the presence of our soul, our well of being and to live freely out of it. Our wisdom tells us that, our fearful, small self needs to be included in this new life. What are we doing for our inner child? In the serious world including our serious life of trying to make important changes, where are our simple joys?

> *What have we done that is fun today? Life's little joys can open big doors in our hearts. It is important to remember, at least one joy every-day.*

## Fine Tuning

The next stage in the unfolding of our souls is the smoothing out of our lives. A harmony is growing. Joy springs from a fountain within us. This source inside leads to deeper joy as our restless thoughts give way to more being. We are building a new home inside for something more profound then momentary pleasures or finding comfort. There is new space for joy, rooms of joy, presence of joy. The muscles of the soul are strengthening, building a life that is more secure then our previous search for security.

This is a time for fine-tuning. What activities, friendships serve the unfolding of my soul and what is merely passing time? How much are my thoughts entertaining unnecessary small talk, gossip, fantasy, and how much are my thoughts present to enjoy life? How much am I wasting my life energy in unnecessary worry and waiting for things to happen? How much am I enjoying the well of peace within and the simple peace around me? What habits am I holding onto because they are simply a habit? What new life is calling me? How much time each day do I give myself for joy? How much time do I give myself to receive the impulse from this joy to my soul? Where is my real commit-ment? What is my intention?

We are finding a new sense of our true self. We are not so dependent upon what others are saying and thinking. We begin to see the people in our lives differently. They are not more important or less important then we are. We see everyone as more innocent. Life is not so complicated. Our daily identity does not have so many extreme highs followed by difficult lows. We discover our equanimity. Our awareness is greater then the obstacles we encounter. What would have really upset us in the past, now we find gently flowing by.

We are not always quite sure if the joy we are finding is nourishing our personality or our soul. What is the difference? How do we know if we are feeding ourselves deeply or just indulging ourselves in little joys? The mind can find so many questions and problems. Meanwhile, joys, big or small, significant or simple are nourishing our being. It is not so important what is being touched, the personality or our souls. We are being touched. We are feeding our hearts. Slowly, our whole being is coming forward. Slowly, our passion, life energy, soul is being felt more.

Our minds are less busy finding questions and problems and more open and receptive to experience. We feel our selves. We are clearer. Real food in the form of a certain teaching, in nature, with a friend, or simply feeling our inner peace is feeding us deeply. We feel a presence inside of us. We feel whole. We feel ourselves. Our lives on the outside are more stable even if our work and relationships are unchanged. We are less fearful. With less fear we are not entangled in unnecessary drama and worry. We are more truthful in every part of life. We feel more and react less to the events around us. We are.

In this period of joy's life, we are not searching so much and simply enjoying life more. The rebuilding of life happened one day at a time. Joy, we realize, was not in the big changes in life but in the little moments. Joy is the river of life that we slowly find again, breathe and create from. The practice of choosing joy has brought realignment in everything we think is important. Relationships, work, daily choices large and small have changed. This realignment also changes the course of the thoughts and feelings, which normally rule our awareness.

Choosing joy is less a pushing away of what are not joy and more recognition of what is joy. It is a learning to say "yes" more then saying "no". The joy that is found naturally pulls forward more joy as the other parts of life recede into the background. People normally project their lack of joy towards their work and relationships. But the answers are not so easy. Unless we have a new foundation of joy, making changes in work and relationships usually just finds new sets of problems. In the life of joy, true work, true relationships naturally unfold. This can be the work and friends already with us changing as we change. Often new work and friends come into our lives to meet our new joy.

The joy is as much in our tears as our smiles. This joy is present in our daily truth and in our sleep. Our dreams become less of a reaction to the day's events and more full of clarity and experiences of expanded being.

> *Life is the dream of our soul awakening.*

What we experience during the day and while asleep at night is connected. We are abundant. Our heart is not alone or separate but interwoven with every soul in our life. Many states of awareness are feeding us. Joy can be found in pain and difficulty as well as success and freedom. Joy is as much in serving others as it is in nurturing a forgotten part of our self.

> *Joy is something that comes from inside of us that spreads throughout our being and extends forever outward. Joy is life experienced fully.*

### Life Is Sacred

The rebuilding of our life is an emptying out. In our remembering, joy calls us to make a space inside ourselves and space outside in our lives, separate from the noise and business of the everyday world. To rebuild, we need space in our lives to allow this to happen. Many people remind themselves of making a space for their soul by keeping a personal altar in their room at home. An altar is a reminder that life is more then doing. Life is sacred. Making an altar is a reminder to make room in our lives for simply being, for the sacred. In every heart is a unique altar to God. Our altar mirrors what we find in our hearts. What we place on the altar is reminding us where we find real food. An altar may include a picture of nature, loved one, teacher or a symbol that touches us at church. The altar may be a flower from the garden and a candle. Any symbol that reminds us of real food is appropriate for our altar. And our altar can change as our joy and experience of our soul changes. When we make a space for our soul, we are reminding our selves, our soul really exists. It is important. It is worth honoring. When we spend time with our altar, the presence is with us, inside of us. We are feeling the space inside where our soul is unfolding. Our joy is rebuilding, finding it own course through the practice of having our attention.

This space becomes natural and normal as we make friends with life's emptiness. Our altar can be our space where we sit and be with our emptiness. Instead of fear restlessly moving, we find something else. Our altar is a reminder there is much more than the struggles we can easily find. We do not have to be compulsively doing. We simply are. Our altar is where we can practice this awareness of being. At the altars in life we find the big difference between a life of being busy and a life of meaning. The altars of life remind us of sacredness. Here we find peace in our emptiness. The altar is where we can explore our ocean of being.

In our finding the absolute, the purity, life's inherent divinity we are less defensive, insecure, and lonely. From the repeated experience of our well of being, we can change our lives, live with vulnerability, and less attachment. In our emptiness, we can behold the exquisite. The beloved, what we have sought for so long is found deep within us. The separation is over. Our small self, our humanness are parts of the grand totality of being. Life has a fundamental intimacy that no promise, no special opportunity can tempt us to abandon. We burn in the well of truth and clarity. We are wedded to the bride/bridegroom within. Our human and divine being have chosen one and other. As in any true love relationship, the honesty and nakedness at times seems to destroy our egos, everything that we know. Meanwhile the veils over our ultimate nature, our lightness of being moves aside.

We find new energy, lots of new energy. Simple activities like eating, walking, talking with friends can be powerful moments, passionate, radiant. The mysteries of the saints and mystics are alive within us. The Divine uniqueness in our souls is unfolding. This happens as our lives are experienced less as being tossed about in the waves of daily life. We are living more in joy's ocean. This new source of energy comes as we stop holding onto pictures of how we think our lives should be. Living free of pictures and more open to what is, gives us our creative source again. Life's precious energy is no longer wasted or working against us. We have found our ground of being. Life is moving for us, with us, in us. Our awareness rests in our true ground inside of us. Here is our security, our shelter, our protection, and refuge. In our great letting go of what is not important, joy has found more room to make a home inside of us and in the world. In our great letting go, life is always changing, renewing. As we find clear sky, a mind free of being busy with thought, our awareness and daily life, become clearer. As we find our fire, our fears grow smaller and our passion larger.

*We let go into the vast ocean of God's presence. In our ground of being we experience life as if we are carried.*

In these later stages of our soul unfolding, we have less of an agenda in life and more simple gratitude. Daily life naturally rises and falls back into our ocean of being. The world we see everyday and enjoy is the great ocean, God in our midst. What is true does not take great effort. There is less need to search for joys in the world. Each day is full of much presence. Everyone in our life is part of God, our soul, our true being. When something good happens to a friend, it is as if it happening to us. We are not separate. Their joys are our joys. Their challenges are ours as well. Their beauty, grace, and unique presence are also parts of us. In joy's vast being, everyone and everything is connected. We see, hear, touch, and feel through our hearts, our heartfulness. God is unfolding into form all around us. Our soul is fresh awareness. God is vitally present. Simply being present has replaced other sources of nourishment. In our daily ordinariness, our profound nothingness is glimpses of a sheltered existence, which gives us faith beyond words. Kindness is life's natural stream. The grass nearby is ever friendly after sitting in our depths of being. Joy is offering completely and receiving deeply. Sitting, dancing, living this presence is the gift we give to the world. It is our soul's gift to us.

# *To Love the Small Self*

Our small self is not God's punishment for being bad. It is not our karma or result of sin. It is not something we must suffer with. Our small self is only the part of us that is separate. We are separate at one time or another from our joy. We step out of our river of truth, our ocean of being. Our small self, our separateness grabs onto pictures of life instead of living life itself. Our small self struggles with our personal story instead of being free to make a new story or let go of our story and just enjoy life.

In comparison with the Divine realms where the presence is complete, perfect with love's pure joy, normal earthly life is full of limits. Our bodies have limits in how we feel and what we can do. Our personalities have limits in our emotional and intellectual capacities. These limitations can be called our small self. Sometimes our small self, including our worries and concerns occupy our entire day. The small self seemingly fills every part of life. In making a life for our soul, there is no way around learning to love our small self, loving our limitations.

What actually is my small self? May be it is only a set of patterns, a behavior, a place we go to inside when no other way is found. May be the small self is nothing but where we are accustomed to touching the ground inside. It is a familiar way of reacting. It may be a pattern, a behavior we learned as a small child which has stuck to us ever since. What we judge as the small self in others and ourselves maybe is nothing, just an old routine that they or we never thought about dropping. Maybe the routine still serves us. Regardless, the small self is not so important. It doesn't need to take up so much of our attention, denial, criticism, or concerns. The energy we give it in our condemnation could be making it more difficult, making it worse then it really is. Our small self is our small self, nothing more or less. It is not an excuse for hurting others or our self. Neither is our small self something bigger or smaller then what it is. Without all the thoughts we have attached to it, it is nothing but an energy we sometimes move into, a space where we live in before joy frees us. The small self invites our love and joy again and again. To bring our hearts into our difficulties, this is joy's calling.

When our children trip and fall we do not make a big occasion out of it. We pick them up, hold them, and let them run off again. Similarly, when our small self trips we can pick him or her up again. We hold him, and let him run off. Our small self has many faces. It is our self-ishness, moodiness, anger, laziness, and unhealthy habits. We can spend our life trying to be rid of him or we can love him, pick him up, hold him, and let him run off again in life's joy. The small self is a part of us as well as our large self. There is no competition between the two. The body has its needs and the personality has its ways. Our soul has its own expression in our life. To realize our soul, we do not need to eliminate the needs of our body and personality. Unfolding our soul into our life is not a life of denial of our human parts. Our sexuality, patterns in eating, relationships, work, all our feelings are gifts to open again and again. Each time our experience is different.

> *Loving the small self, we begin to see the perfection of being born in this body with this personality and our soul. They are all me!*

## A Survivor in Need of Love

People can spend all their energy trying to look away, to conquer, or to control their small self, hoping it will behave the way he or she should. Or we can spend our energy living the best of our physical, emotional, intellectual capacity. Joy is the true healer. Joy gives perspective. Joy gives and gives to the small self, which is in need of lots and lots of love. Our small self is a survivor. Our childhood experiences formed our small self into a personality that managed the best it could against the pressures and demands of growing up. Our culture puts a blanket of fear and expectation over the purity of our hearts. Our souls wait for life's pure joy to re-emerge. Now we are called to find heartfulness, understanding, compassion, and forgiveness for all our limits. We are called to offer a committed love, a sincere love to heal the separation from our full being, the river of joy inside. Loving our small self leads us to naturally have more heartfulness, understanding, and love for the small self of others.

Normally we quickly judge our small self-including our patterns in relationships, work, our lack of self-control, our quick temper or stubbornness. We easily judge our desires including our sexuality. Our judgements of our small self can be more punishing and destructive then the actual behavior or desires. There is often a truth worth learning in what we call our small self. Our patterns of behavior may be telling us that we are living a path that is too far from our hearts, our truth.

> Our small self is the limited ground we live upon instead of our true ground of being. Our small self is what we are told and believe that we deserve. We deserve much more!

Instead of punishing ourselves for having a small self, it maybe more important to find again our inspiration and joy. Our distractions, habits, and moods may be the way our small self tries to protect itself from the world, from others who do not understand. What we call our small self may be our sensitivity that is protecting our inner child and, our feelings that need to be listened to and cared for. If we listened to and acknowledged our desires, they can lead us to our deeper desires, someplace richer in our hearts. May be our desires are just an expression of freedom, movement, our energy finding a way to be expressed. Instead of punishing ourselves we are called to receive ourselves. When we feel the energy of who we are without judgement this is liberation.

What we call our small self is a part of us, a part of our hearts. There are many rooms in the heart. We have a small self, a true self, and a no self. There is a well of being inside each of us. There are worlds and worlds of love's vast being inside to explore. But in our conflict with our smaller selves, these worlds remain closed and only open with great difficulty. In the conflicts and judgements we project on to others and ourselves we limit the exploration. The doors to the other rooms inside, our greater aspects are limited. Joy opens the sacred inner doors. In joy, our awareness can move from anger to peace, stubbornness to soft heart. We can move from, seemingly out of control desires to simple being. Joy is the highway, the great unifier of the many parts of us. We are not called to battle ourselves, to defeat parts of us, and hope other parts dominate and prevail. There is more to life then heroes, being tough and strong. We are also gentle, loving, accepting, and giving. In our offering of everything in our hearts and receiving we are boldly human. Every part of our small self is a part of our being and has a purpose. Sometimes we are ecstatic energy. At times we are small, crowded inside with frustration and anger. A short time later we may be soft again with no thoughts, just feeling a vast space of peacefulness. Joy lets the energy move.

# The True Self

There is the small self and there is true self. The true self is our freed awareness. This awareness extends beyond our personal story, beyond our personality. When the river of our awareness is not full of thoughts and emotions, worries and wishes, we find ourselves in a vast space extending without limit. Even when our mind is clouded with thoughts it is possible to perceive the whole mind. The sun of our soul is present. There is a vast inner sky without clouds, without thoughts. As we learn to let the clouds, our thoughts, drift by and not catch our attention, we are at the doors to our true self. True self is fresh awareness. We are living instead of planning. We are fully being instead of reacting and preparing. Our true self is the expression of millions of small lights of our nerve endings. Our true self is inexplicably interwoven in the pure lightness of our essence that includes all beings, nature, the stars and galaxies.

*Our soft awareness is our ground of being.*

## The Intimate Being

The true self begins again and again as real food gives its impulse to life for our soul. As we receive the impulse, we find and explore this vast space. It is warm and inviting. The further our awareness goes into our heart center, the more peace and light we discover. Our heart space opens to layers or levels of beautiful intimacy, this is the Intimate Being. As we let go and are not grasping with our fears and wishes, another self opens to us. It is a self without borders. Here we experience our awareness growing, expanding through us, spreading larger in and beyond our bodies. Our awareness continues to expand around us,

162

in the room, growing through the walls, going outside, expanding until we realize there is no end. Our true self is as a vast body. It is our spiritual body, joy's home. It is our home without walls. Through meditation, we realize our opportunity to discover and enjoy our true self, our true body. Our awareness and the stars and galaxies are no longer experienced separately. Our true self, the identity we carry into eternity is not separate, but includes all there is.

This understanding only comes from experience. We cannot intellectually arrive at this awareness. It is living in our heart, our inner being, where our awareness unfolds in this intimate experience. Meanwhile, we have not lost or overcome our small self. Our everyday identity, our feelings and concerns, even our bad habits or personal difficulties are still with us. Our true self lives with and beyond our everyday personality. There is no battle for triumph over ourselves. Our small self remains but we are no longer so compulsively identified with it. We are our thoughts and feelings and we know some part of us that is more. We can be in this vast awareness and at the same moment or soon afterwards be in our thoughts and desires. Our small self, our busy thoughts, often remain present but they are not so strong as to distract us. Our small self, although present, is not preventing us from knowing our true being.

> *We understand our normal identity is clothing for our awareness to be in this world.*

After knowing our true self, we see the small self differently. It does not rule as before. There is an alternative. We are more. The large self includes our identification with something more. The trees, flowers, sunsets, and stars are part of the same being. The small self that struggles for recognition and little fulfillments is just one part of us. There is the true self that seemingly has no body but is pure satisfaction. It is our ground of vast being. Life is awareness, peace. While the small self tries to control, manage, and direct everything around, the true self has no need to control. We simply want to experience what life presents. The little self is fearful. It resists and reacts. Our large self is a shelter, a refuge, our original home that is beyond words. We resist or react less to what life brings to us. In truth we are free.

We can recognize the difference. The small self talks and lives effectively in this world. But we know this activity is ultimately limited. It is the small self that is busy doing, maintaining, surviving. Meanwhile our true self is a mountain of being, gardens of pure presence, living in the heartfulness of eternity's body. We each have our own experience that gives us the words. This experience changes our idea of life's meaning and purpose. Our awareness is connected to something beneath, interwoven, beyond the events of daily life. We are anchored in something profound calling us again and again to experience more.

*Our true self is anchored in our ground of unlimited being.*

## *Exploring Other Dimensions*

We understand we are what we identify with. If we only identify with our small self in its normal world, this is our identity. But when we identify with the true self, there is also another world. Slowly we identify with the greater world. We know it as our true identity. We have both a small self and greater self. Sometimes we are lost in one or found in the other. Joy's path is the healing. Our awareness still shrinks into the concerns and fears organized in our small self. However, joy also expands into seeing our greater body and experiencing the vastness. From this perspective, we see the push and pull of our small self as temporary, without substance, empty in its true nature.

As our large self is experienced, the small struggles, while still present take less of our energy and attention. We see, hear, and know that our true self is our ocean of being. The waves may separate our awareness into challenge and difficulty but the ocean is not far away. Our personality, our small self is the personal machinery we have to navigate our everyday world. Meanwhile we are exploring other dimensions. The small self may be necessary machinery, nothing to really disturb or be unloving towards. Our ideas, feelings, desire, and concerns all help navigate and manage our physical life. From the inside our true self slowly illuminates every thought, lifts every feeling, opens every inspiration, as we are more of our true nature.

*Our true self empowers us, enlivens us, transforming our perceived limitations. Our true self fills our awareness with a generosity of spirit, a sweet stillness, an expectation of life to mirror the intimacy we find inside. Our true self gives our small self a place to rest, to be embraced. Golden threads are weaving into all our awareness and activities, in all realms, that our lives adventure into.*

# The No Self

Before our awareness contracted into self, joy's natural body was a soft open no self. Before we divided into our small and greater self in our growing up, we were our no self. In our separation from the pure joy, our thoughts separated from our feelings and our heart separated from our soul.

> *Our no self is the end of our separation. It is awareness without observer, without self-reflection.*

Underneath our normal life of worry and stress, we have a place of no duality, no separation. Real food is an impulse to remember ourselves before the separation. It is an impulse for pure being, being our no self. Real food nourishes something inside of us that is more than our thoughts, more than our feelings. Real food brings us back to joy's river. When we are submerged in this river there is only joy. There is nothing else, only our no self. As we receive, as we are this joy, the self that we live each day is seen for what it is. It is empty. There is no self. We are joy's being. Our thoughts rise out of our being. From our thoughts come feelings, relationships, tasks, activities, the daily life we give meaning to everyday. Everything comes from the no self. Everyday we begin again. We give meaning to the thoughts entering our awareness. Our thoughts build into relationships and activities. Out of our no self our world is born again and again. When we reach this awareness, our no self, we find our whole being before we fit into our everyday identity. During the day, we remember our no self, our whole being. We are so much more then the tight suit of this worldly identity we assume. We are so much more then the waves and currents of our daily life. This no self is our soul, joy's endless body.

Our no self shows us how we are creating our daily world. Out of our no self, we attach significance, stress, expectation, and disappointment to the events of our lives. Being in our no self, we learn not to so quickly leap into our normal identity. Be. Be for a while. We feel our expanded being. The daily world will still be there after we bathe in this body of joy, our no self. No self is reminding us of our original innocence, our soul's body before we squeeze our being into our daily life. No self is our naked awareness, the crisp, lucid freshness of life itself. Our no self rests in our being welcomed home inside surrounded in meadows of wild flowers. We find this experience in our hearts.

Most people never rest. They are always carrying the weight and demands of their daily self, the thoughts and feelings that seemingly have no end. They do have an end. The no self is greater then all the tasks and demands we take for granted. Every moment of real food is an impulse to remember our no self. The experience of our vast being helps us to collect all the energy we are projecting out into the world. We bring this projection back inside and rest in our no self. Much of our life energy is put into relationships and work. We can recollect and restore our energy in our no self. Our no self is pure, without categories, conditions, nothing hidden, everything present.

## *The Empty Mind*

Remembering our no self is a path of remembering to not attach our awareness so quickly and so strongly to the worries and desires, the challenges and difficulties we find. It is a path of remembering to be present in our well of being. It is a path of silence, resting our awareness in its vast, natural landscape. There is no need for entertainment, to seek more comfort. There is no need to do anything, have anything, to think. Our no self is one with everything inside and outside of us.

Our no self grows in our awareness as we practice offering self in this moment and receive our no self in its spaciousness. When we are no self, we are free. We have more to give. When we are our no self, we are not acting and reacting to life out of fear or unnecessary wishes. We are present in our simple awareness. We are present. No self is simple awareness without identifying, any thoughts and feelings. Many people think its normal for the mind to be always busy. But in fact, the mind is naturally empty, no-self, clear sky. Years of living with fear and chasing desires in our mind has clouded our no self. Our habit of false identification has changed including our projection of life's security into the daily world. It is our culture's belief that the physical world is all that is real, that the answers are outside of us, that God is separate from us, that makes a busy mind. The natural mind, our no self is empty. When there is a need to think, we think. The mind is like any other muscle. It doesn't need to be busy unless it is needed. Under everything we carry in our hearts, our no self shines, radiates its own lucid being. In our innocence our no self expands through and beyond our body, beyond all limits.

Our no self is abundant in perfect quiet and a rest from life's sometimes overwhelming noise. Our no self, our soul unfolds naturally when received. Our no self is the absolute that gives complete security. As we let the world and all its activity be outside, we discover a groundless ground of being inside, God's presence. This groundless ground of being is solid in its pure clarity. God is the perfect ground inside of us, our no self. The brilliance of the love, the exquisite texture of the peace grows in the softness and innocence recovered in our hearts.

The no self unfolds within our hearts as the psychic layers of unnecessary thoughts and feelings peel away in joy's loving embrace. In joy's healing our no-self reaffirms God's fundamental being. Our no self is the passing from an identity of "I want" to another perception of being the totality of life. Our awareness occupies a space that is ultimate, clean, and pure, both empty and full of sweetness. Our awareness spreads through and beyond the content of our life.

Why constantly be in our identity as parent, partner, professional, and so on? Why should we live in the tight suit of our worldly self? This is not who we really are. This worldly identity we take so seriously will all change and someday drop away completely. Why not enjoy bathing in our naked awareness, our inner joy, our no self? Here we are not busy making an identity. We are not exhausted projecting our identity, our life energy in the world. We are experiencing life in its simple presence. The no self does not find life complicated. We are present.

Our no self is a gift for everyone around us. They too will take their costume, the roles they play less seriously. They too may let go of struggles and attachments, disappointments and expectations more easily. Perhaps they too will find the joy present in the moment. This moment is the door to the no self. Being present doesn't require any self, any training, motivation, preparation, or adjustment. Young children are often in their no self, directly experiencing life. It is in our culture, in education we fail to support the children to keep their no self, their open mind, soft heart. We take away their no self in the name of educating them. When in truth we should honor their no self and then teach them a worldly identity. We should remind them this worldly identity is important but they are more. Their no self is their true nature, pure and beautiful. Imagine education honoring the innocence, simple being of the children. Imagine teachers supporting the children to trust, enjoy, and rest in their pure being. The children would quickly find this place inside, underneath their thoughts and feelings. They would naturally find their no self. Our inner world has value. The no self is important. There is no competition.

*We can be intelligent and productive in the world and remember our no self. We fail to see that we are both.*

We are a no self and we have a unique personality and physical life. The no self is our lucid, carefree being which is the source of our intuition, our creativity, and our passion. Our no self is our connection to the sacred. It is our home, shelter, and refuge.

Everything sacred grows and blossoms in this selfless presence. The sacred is not in our ideas but in our direct experience of the peace, the dimensions of love, in this presence of no time and no effort. The no self is the garden of God's being inside of us and in the world. The no self gives birth to all aspects of our being. Our nerves, imagination, and heart are fueled with life's nectar. This nectar is experienced in the depths of our heart, in the depths of our no self. The sweetness of life, the relaxed presence is the perfume of our essence, our no self. This nectar is natural. It is life itself. From this nectar everything good grows in our being and in our life. Remembering our no self is to remember this nectar, life's inherent sweetness. This oneness, our being beyond being is the soil of life's garden. This soil has unlimited fertility, life. It is abundance without end.

Our worldly self will return. But in the times of no self, in these intimate moments, there is a special opportunity. We want to recognize the no self. This is holy time.

> We want to practice seeing, hearing, tasting, touching, and knowing
> life directly through the heart. This is when God is very present.

Life's sacred times stay always with us; even when worldly demands and struggles again occupy our consciousness and life. Somewhere our no self is always present. No self is who we are. Separation has become joy.

# V. New Paradigm

# *Meditation*

Meditation helps us to end the separations. Our small self, true self, no self are all parts of us. Where one begins and another ends is not so important. We are one person. It is beautiful how the same heart can be so contracted in one moment and moments later seemingly extend to the stars and the planets. This acceptance of every part of us, every aspect of life comes from awareness of our soul. Our ground of being includes everything in our inner garden. Meditation brings us to this awareness of true ground. It is inside of us. Meditation is simple remembering. Our ground of being calls us.

> *Slowly, our thoughts and feelings, what we do and how we live is becoming connected again. Everything in life is coming from, growing naturally out of our ground of being. Meditation is coming inside, resting at home again, in our own special room.*

(Specific meditations are given in the appendix.)

## *Time to Be*

In the modern world where what we do is what is important. Meditation slows our awareness to being in the midst of all our doing. By definition, taking the time to be, we find the spirit of heartfulness that leads us to understanding. Slowly the other qualities of forgiveness, compassion, and wisdom help us to find clarity about what is true and what is only a distraction. Our wisdom tells us to stay with our fire, passion, our truth. Meditation is our time to be.

Taking time to sit, simply, and do nothing can be the most important time of each day. Instead of our mind wandering off into worry or search for comforts we really do not need, meditation brings us back to our ground of being. This is our source of security that our identity can fully take root in. This is what holds a restless mind and calms nervous energy.

In the busy world, meditation affirms us. The simple act of sitting is a reminder to be present, feeling life's presence inside and around us. As busy as the mind is with thoughts during meditation, this is a reminder of how busy our awareness is generally. Meditation is not a time to be busy creating, visualizing, wanting something to happen. Meditation is our time to be present to all there is inside our hearts. Slowly, the thoughts become less and our awareness greater. In meditation we let go of everything pulling our awareness someplace other than where we are. We let go. In the simplicity of our naked heart, meditation begins. Innocence is present. It is who we are. There are no techniques, which quicken the process. What is being hurried? Our thoughts and feelings tangled and wrapped around our activity in the world slowly unravel. Like peeling an onion, meditation is coming back, returning, closer and closer to our true self one layer at a time. In worldly life, our identity is full of activity, thoughts and feelings. In meditation we are remembering we are something more.

Simply being aware of our heart, our breathing, we feel our own life energy. Every time we stop and become aware helps us to take back the big projection, the projection we are constantly making outside in the world. Life is here, inside of us. Meditation is remembering. Meditation returns us to life and life's natural vulnerability. Our anxiety about the difficulties lessens as we simply sit. Our fears about what will happen decrease as we take this time to be present. All the different energies from work, relationships, the noisy life become slowly quiet, still. We feel ourselves again.

*Meditation everyday is an opportunity to feel ourselves, our own presence, the preciousness of God inside and around us.*

Meditation is loving our awareness whether clear or cloudy with lots of thoughts and feelings. Meditation is loving our awareness in this moment.

*In meditation we become available again.*

## Not Another Task to Master

In the beginning, meditation is just a time to observe how busy and unquiet we are. We want to get up and do something. This is okay. An important step in finding our peacefulness is to see how busy we are. Meditation is not something to conquer. It is not how long we sit or how still we are that gives the answers. Sitting a few minutes and then changing positions is fine. Slowly, slowly the muscle inside of heartfulness is strengthening. The mind relaxes. The breath eases. Our awareness begins to find space inside, a soft place. Meditation brings us to new awareness of our soft being. We begin to feel something pulling us further inside. Something is present welcoming us, inviting us. Inside is our fire, our passion. Our heart is more then a beating muscle but has empty room, peace, colors, feelings we did not know before. Meditation may appear as the same exercise everyday but in fact everyday is different. There is something new to find inside every time we take the time to come to our special silence.

We look forward to the time each day when we can simply be inside and remember. Meditation is remembering the ground of being. The world around is fading into the background as awareness travels inside, journeying past thoughts and concerns, emotions, our mental traffic. It is only traffic. Underneath the busy mind, around it, in the midst of it is our no self. Meditation is the direct experience of the no self. Our awareness has been for so long pushed and shaped outside into the world for meaning and purpose. Now it is important to allow awareness to travel inside us, as deeply as it can go. We let our awareness fall deeply in the heart, the soft spaces we find. Every time, we meditate we relax and let awareness go further within to explore. The mind rests in inner seas of vast space. Awareness glides by passing thoughts, going down through mental layers of distraction, down to pure being. We find true ground, the ground of I. I am.

From this ground, life's activity, relationships, and projects begin and end. From this ground we see clearly. We know what is true and what is just being busy. What parts of life grow from one's ground of true being and what is merely a product of restless thoughts and wishes? From the ground of being, we hear, touch, and feel. Meditation brings awareness to what has true roots, real meaning. And meditation reveals what is not important, mere activity. Meditation is finding the soil inside us from which everything in life grows and develops. By feeling our awareness in this soil; the weeds of life, what is old and just taking space, what is new and needs attention, all becomes clear.

*Meditation is being close to life at its very beginning, its essence.*

*We get inner strength in meditation. Every time we sit inside, we sail again in the seas of eternity and the world outside is not so controlling.*

Every time we sail effortlessly in meditation, our awareness learns to let go and glide past unnecessary thoughts and concerns and our rising and falling emotions. Our awareness is washed clean. We rest deep inside beneath our fears including any darkness we find. This darkness, these fears, separate us, like a cover over our well of being. Underneath this realm of thought is the calm heart, our source. Letting go into our inner well, further in the calm heart, we find our light, our lightness of being. Here there is no polarity. There is no struggle between good and evil. In our well of being, our essence is only goodness. No matter how much difficulty and complexity we have build on top of it, our well of being is endless peace.

We find our goodness naturally as we remember who we are in meditation. We see clearly our self, true self, the no self. Joy is our core being, life's essence. We see the ocean of eternity and our normal world taking shape and growing out of it. Meditation, the practice of letting go and dissolving into the empty place inside is how we find our true home again and again. Like an onion unraveling, our awareness opens to itself, clinging less, attaching less, softening to its true nature. Meditation is the path of freedom; free of form, free of attachments, free of desire, free of the complicated self.

> *Meditation by its very nature heals and opens, simplifies, and purifies. Meditation and our ground of being help us to be true in every part of life.*

The large space we find inside helps us to find more space in daily life. This space gives us room to be true to the moment. As meditation frees us of compulsive, clinging thoughts, we are freer in our actions and reactions in the world. Our awareness is empowered. We find our very essence, the fuel of life, our perfect ground of being.

Every time we meditate we begin again. No matter what our lives were like a few minutes before, each meditation gives us the possibility to be completely new. In the simple ground inside we are all possibility, all potential. As others are grounded in their work, partnership, family, or worldly activity, we become grounded in the space inside of nothingness and everything. This space gives freedom to be new in every part of life. Life can change because we are not holding onto any thought, belief, anyone or thing as the focus of our identity. Meditation gives us the fertile ground of life itself.

# *Having Intentions*

As meditation supports our inner life, our intentions support our life in the world. As meditation helps free us from unnecessary inner traffic, our intentions help free us of unnecessary busy-ness in life. Meditation and our intentions teach us to be more and do less. They support us to live what is true for us.

> *Our intentions are the extension of our meditation after we have risen from sitting and go into our normal lives.*

Intentions can be the bridge for the inner and outer life. They can be the bridge from our small to our large self. Intentions can be the bridge from the life of many desires coming from our personality and culture to the life of fewer, deeper desires which express our life's essence and our pure being. Intentions are our personal guides instead of following what everyone else is doing.

## *Helping Us in Knowing What to Do*

Everyday we have choices to make. How do we know what is ultimately best for us? How do we know if our desire for bigger and more is just our small self-speaking inside of us or the truth? For example, how do we know if we need a bigger house or smaller house? Is this our small self-seeking our big self with a projection of having a larger home? Do we really need a larger house? Maybe we need an extra room for a future project. And maybe a bigger house is just more to pay and care for. How do we know? Similarly, is a job offering more income just leading to a life of more stress or maybe an important opportunity to have the income necessary for the future? From where are our decisions coming from everyday? Are we listening to our intellect, our fears, our hearts, or our joy? How do we know?

Everyday life can so quickly turn in unexpected or unwanted directions. There are so many distractions, different voices to respond to. How do we know where to turn? How do we know where to go? What will support our soul unfolding in our life? What is just another detour keeping us separate from our true joy? Intentions are the bridge where our awareness remembers our ground of being, where we find renewal. This is the bridge to our true self, our soul. Our intentions call forth our highest qualities. These qualities come from our soul, through our hearts, and out into our lives. Through our intentions, our soul can grow and expand in our hearts and daily life.

> *Through having intentions, our soul is supported and guided into the world.*

Most people do not live with clear intentions. They are just living reacting to the circumstances of each day. They live the changing whims of their personality. One day we can desire one thing and the next want something entirely different. Many people may have goals for themselves for achievements, for success. But goals for worldly accomplishments are not the same as intentions to be our true selves and joy.

Traditionally in many religions and cultures, those committed to listening to the calling of their souls took spiritual vows of poverty, chastity, and obedience. They would leave normal society and enter the world of a monastery or ashram. The community away from normal society would be a big support. However, more often then not, the inner struggles and victories were the same whether someone was wearing robes or was living in normal clothes in the world. Poverty is not holding on tightly our worldly possessions, who we think we are. Poverty includes allowing the heart to breathe and let go of fixed ideas and the pictures we carry in our minds. Chastity is to remember the pure place inside of us, our golden self. Chastity may or may not include celibacy. The two have become confused. Many communities close the door to sexuality on the outside but like most people, they still must find a place for their sexuality or life energy within themselves. Chastity is more about remembering God's pure being in our souls than trying to control or master our passions. Obedience reminds us not to be distracted by all the different voices we hear, but to remember to seek our truth.

Vows or intentions are an ancient way to find a bridge for unfolding our souls in our lives. Traditional vows for many are too impersonal and joyless. Instead we are choosing intentions, which honor our joy, our essence, the qualities of our soul. We choose intentions to remind us who we want to be in the world. Our calling of joy may include remembering simplicity, peace, innocence, or gentleness. It may include remembering love, passion, or honesty. We can take intentions for heartfulness, understanding, compassion, or forgiveness. Our intentions are daily reminders while we are making decisions where to go, whom to meet, how to be and react to life around us.

Our intentions are sources of joy. They literally help keep us close to our hearts and the hearts of others.

*Intentions remind us of our inner river. Instead of being side tracked by attractions that are not really right for us, our intentions bring us back to our center. Instead of being tossed back and forth by the waves of daily life, intentions remind us of our great ocean of being.*

### Possible Intentions

| | |
|---|---|
| Simplicity | Obedience |
| Humility | Humor |

| | |
|---|---|
| Perfect joy | Play |
| Dignity | Honesty |
| Honor | Patience |
| Passion | Understanding |
| Purity | Silence |
| Innocence | Solitude |
| Surrender | Love |
| Gratitude | Strength |
| Peace | Courage |
| Goodness (in everything) | Contentment |
| Forgiveness | Compassion |
| Giving | Service |
| Prayer | Gentleness |
| Tenderness | Reverence |
| Being | Creativity |
| Poverty | Devotion |
| Beauty | Bliss |
| Chastity | Friendship |
| Trust | To Be |

The intentions we choose are reminders of our experience of joy. For each of us, they are a little different. We each can choose intentions that feel the closest to how we experience our essence. This is our true joy, to feel our essence. For someone this is when he or she remembers gratitude. When they take the time to remember gratitude, their thanksgiving fills their entire body and they feel whole. For someone else, it is when they remember their innocence, or to play. When they take the time to remember their innocence and play, the day if very different. For someone else their joy is always close when they remember gentleness with themselves and gentleness with others. Someone else finds their real joy when they remember devotion. This devotion is to God, their soul. Devotion can be in all the little moments in each day. Someone else remembers joy, when they hold life in reverence or when they remember giving. When they give more and expect less, they feel their souls very present. Many people come closer to their joy when they remember their passion, to be creative, or remember their bliss.

For one person it maybe important to be humble. For someone else it may be truer to have more strength to speak up and be honest. For someone else, joy comes when they remember to pray and remember their faith. Others find their joy by remembering to discover a moment of peace or many moments of peace. Some people easily fall into deep joy when they remember to take time for their solitude. For someone else it may be taking time for serving others. Simplicity seems to bring almost everyone to their essence, their ground of being. Beauty or humor are prefect remedies for a serious world in which it is difficult to remember joy.

### *Honoring Our Truth*

In our path of pursuing real food, we soon know which intentions bring us closer and which further from the joy we are seeking. When choosing intentions it is best and clearest, when we choose three intentions. The first is truth.

> *We want to be, listen, and honor our truth. To be true to ourselves, true to our path is an intention for us all. The intention of truth is the foundation for unfolding our soul in our life.*

Our second and third intention, each come from our own truth. They could be joy, peace, or love, simplicity, or surrender and passion. These second and third intentions may come from the list above. Or maybe this list inspires us to find other intentions. Perhaps we find a quality that feels more in tune with our way of experiencing joy. Which intentions will lead us to more joy as how we know it? This joy is our essence. When we are living closer to our essence, we are unfolding our souls, God in our lives. The intentions we choose help us heal our separation. Someone may choose intentions of truth, simplicity, and joy. It may be just right for someone to choose truth, humility and courage. Truth, peace, and contentment are intentions for others. The three intentions work together. For example, truth is to remember our peace and contentment. My peace comes when I remember my truth and contentment. Contentment is certain, as I remember my truth and peace. When we have three intentions, each supports the other. They make a perfect triangle. Each person chooses the intentions which bring them closest to their full being, the being they are yearning for, themselves. Intentions are meant as gifts not obligations. Each person chooses the three greatest gifts they would want for their lives right now. Each intention is a gift to remember to open and enjoy each day.

Intentions can be taken for one month or six months. Intentions can be taken for a year or three years. They can be taken for life. What is important is that our intentions are alive, real. What is important is that our intentions are true, that they are supporting us to unfold our souls in our lives.

## *Guiding Our Daily Decisions*

> *After choosing three intentions, we practice receiving our intentions inside of us and in our daily life. It is important to keep our intentions in front of our awareness.*

We want to wake each day and remember each evening our intentions. The intentions for example; truth, simplicity, peace, all are lamps for our awareness. Our intention is our guide in making decisions, the many choices before us. The intention is a reminder of what is important and where we want to be with our awareness. Our intentions bring us to the true essence each day. While others have goals for success and various achievements, the intention for example, truth, simplicity, peace, goes to the heart of life itself. Our intentions guide our daily appointment book, our activities, our prayers. Does this relationship give me peace? Is it true for me now in my life? Does the relationship make my life simple or more complicated? If not, we ask if there is enough value to pursue the relationship anyway. Remembering truth, simplicity, peace helps evaluate every part of life. The intentions guide us to look for these aspects in all activities. Each intention is our guide, hope, the friend we have to take a new view of our life.

Intentions, for example, truth, simplicity, and peace as a daily reminder can erase years of needless sacrifice and compromise. Who am I living for? This is the hidden potential in each intention. Life is short. When we finish this life what is more important then a life of truth, simplicity, and peace? Do we want hearts full of fear and worldly activity or hearts where our souls are unfolding?

> *Our intentions clear the road to our joy in life, to the joy of Heaven. Earth and Heaven are connected in our intentions.*

Joy is joy in all its dimensions. How do people expect to open to the pure joy of eternity when they are depressed and angry about their life circumstances?

To appreciate and value the gift of life is nothing less then living with joy. With joy as our intention, each conversation, each event, the day's many moments, are lived in the light of joy. With our intentions, we are coming closer and closer to the pure essence of our hearts and the heart in everyone we are living with. Life is not wasted away in mere activity. Our intentions are inspiring us and those around us. Joy inspires more joy.

Our intentions shed light on all the excuses we have, to live something other then our truth, our passion, innocence, gratitude, peace, or love. The life of joy begins with holding the intention. Our soul and the presence of God in all forms resonate with our true being. Our essence is supported by the very nature of life everywhere.

# The Extraordinary Becomes the Ordinary.

When we live with intentions that honor our essence, the extraordinary becomes the ordinary. When we have the intentions of joy, love, peace, what is an occasional experience for others, can become normal life. Our intentions set a road map for our souls to unfold in our lives. The life of our souls is extraordinary by definition. We are so much joy, beauty, and life waiting to be experienced and expressed.

When our awareness is grounded in the life of our soul, we may know and sense things before they happen and feel things routinely that others do not normally feel. Others are limited because their awareness is attached to their pictures of how life must look. Their needs and judgments restrict their experience because for them their world must be a certain way. They are attached to how their work, relationships, and the world around them looks. This attachment makes it difficult to see what is. Their identity projected upon the world, limits remembering their inner awareness and the scope of their knowing. As most people are busy talking about something other then what is happening in this moment, they are separate from the wonders of life.

*As we remember to live in this moment of joy the extraordinary is present without limit.*

## The River Is Perfect

The extraordinary is very ordinary for the joyful because we have found our inner world whole and complete. Daily life naturally flows and compliments this inner harmony. We know the inner river will naturally flow its course to the perfect destination. This is the law of the universe, which we come to know and recognize from personal experience. From our process of remembering we find again and again the perfect solution. The right answer is never far away and comes and comes again. The river of life has its own course. And when we live in this river, the next turn or curve is not so difficult to make or even predict.

Equally important, we do not need to know and predict life's next steps. We are secure in the present. We do not need affirmation so much from others when we find affirmation in life itself, in our well of being.

> *The true extraordinary experience is how ordinary we feel. How beautifully simple and true life is.*

We may or may not have visions, dreams, signs, coincidences, pointing us in our heart's direction. Living our heart is enough. The river is so perfect just as it is right now.

As we react less to what has happened and less concerned with what will be, we are discovering more about what is. Life opens within and around us in its true beauty. Relationships are more then two personalities passing each other. Each relationship is two souls touching one another uniquely, becoming stronger in their own being. The depths of love and joy in our sharing are without limit. Living in our river of joy, we are not projecting our fears into the world and the lives of others. We see, hear, and know who we are and those who are with us. This includes the spirits, the presence of beings around us. We naturally feel the love of ones passed to the other side visiting us. In our joy, we can accept the love of angels and Divine presence with us and in us.

*As we grow in joy's body, it is natural to see and hear, to heal and transform ourselves and others with the wealth of love we find. Love naturally moves mountains especially if the mountains have a base of fear.*

Joy's visions, healing, and miracles do not make us special. Love is special. Joy is the nerve endings of the Creator. Joy is the hidden network of the cosmos. The stars literally vibrate in our being. We are intimately connected to all life in joy. Joy is the nectar of the Divine in everyone and everything.

When we are head over heels in love, joy's full dimensions are clear, without doubt. But we have to be head over heels, or in other words, turned upside down from our normal awareness, to remember life's true ecstasy. For more people the great love they find does not last because they do not know how to live turned upside down in their normal reality. This path is joy's calling. Soon everything we hold as true and important is opposite than what we previously thought was true and important. Joy has lifted us to our true dimension.

## *The Spiritual Ego*

It is important not to make love's wonders too special. We do not want to make another personality out of our new life. After letting go of our attachments why would we want to become attached to a new identity, even if joyful. Joy calls us not to take ourselves too seriously. Many people can get caught in the trap of getting rid of one ego only to build another. A spiritual ego is still an ego wanting attention, to control, and afraid to let go into emptiness. The extraordinary is ordinary. It always was and will be. The problem was that we were too busy living separate from ourselves to notice. Our souls are unfolding on God's extraordinary path for us.

Joy's being is naturally full of service to others because this is what brings joy. Service is not an obligation, something we should do, something others expect or want. Service is being in our river of being that naturally flows to the river of others to make them bigger and flow more easily and true. Service is not necessarily in the big projects we have in mind but in the small moments when we are giving from our hearts. Joy naturally lifts everyone around us in joy.

Some people think it is too depressing to be around depressed people. They are afraid they will lose their joy. They are afraid of taking on the other's sadness. The problem is not the other's energy, but our own fear. Our fear is limiting our joy including the joy of being with those who are needy. Giving to others is not joining them in their problems. Nor is giving to others trying to change them with our joy. Giving is simply taking the time, being ourselves with others. We cannot lose our selves. Our joy is who we are. Our river of life cannot be taken from us. Being in our river of life gives others the support to remember. Service is reminding others, joy is never far away.

# *We Are A Soul*

The life of the soul is uncharted territory. Each of us has our own unique inner map including past realms of being, present opportunities, and a future course. Our soul is the frontier that offers the doors to life's real treasure. As joy heals our separation we connect to dimensions of being beyond our imagination or idea of what is possible. This frontier is to dance exquisitely in the gardens of the heart. The journey is to live vigorously and sometimes dangerously on the edges of normal awareness, common reality. The path threatens everything the mind is attached to. As love's fullness unfolds within us, anything that is not true must depart from our life. We must give up everything to have everything, to be nothing to be all. Sometimes we feel completely lost before we discover how much of ourselves is really found. Everything foreign that occupies the heart must fall away as our soul reaches through our life. The path puts us in the footsteps of the mystics and spiritual pilgrims of all faiths who have risked everything for true joy and bliss.

Each of us has our own calling and journey.

> *Once the mind surrenders to the heart and the heart softens to feel its depths, the soul naturally opens and unfolds.*

The course that follows is not something that can be organized, planned, and mapped out. Under the pressures of worldly life, the heart can feel shrunken like a deflated balloon. The soul has disappeared somewhere inside. Receiving the love, peace, gentleness, and purity in our hearts, the balloon begins inflating and growing again.

The awareness of being a soul grows along with it. As the demands of the world can make us feel small, the awareness of our soul gives us an awareness of being the fullness of the universe.

*Many people think the purpose of their life is their personal story, how much they accomplish, their family joys, life's highs and lows coming together in some cosmic scale. But the soul reveals another purpose. We are here to receive our true self, our no self. We are here to receive and enjoy our essence, God inside and all around us.*

The soul is not something we can study or learn about from others. Each of us calls forth our own spirit, our own joy. The voice inside remembers. We are each remembering in our own special way. We can never listen too much.

## *The Perfect Circumstances*

This is life's challenge to receive our true essence through and around and in between life's story. When we understand this, we realize the current circumstances of our lives are perfect. They call for a radical new view. Our life is not by accident, coincidence, or for passing time while we wait for change. The circumstance of our present life is the perfect environment to realize our true self, our no self, our soul. The joys invite our complete awareness, our total embrace. The challenges invite us to our fullness of being. The soul is like an innocent child that we want to recognize, protect, listen to, honor and receive. Our commitment to this child, the awareness of God within us, bears delicious fruit. The sweetness is ours, beyond anything this world can offer or destroy.

In joy's softness and acceptance, the soul opens and unfolds. As our life is nurtured with real food, this joy, this "yes" opens a space inside where the soul expands and takes root in our being. We have the awareness, "I am a soul." This experience is a profound acceptance inside. Sometimes it is an experience of feeling fully rested. It is a space that begins in our inner depths and expands beyond our bodies, expanding seemingly forever. The awareness of the soul is feeling at home. It is a knowing of true self, a self without boundaries, the no self. For some the experience is unending peace or a light that grows as we surrender to it. As the soul opens further, more is revealed. There are worlds and worlds inside the soul's reality. Each person finds his or her our own uniqueness, God's special presence inside. The love is like being the only one in the universe, loved by God. This love does not make our heads big with self-importance but our hearts strong with self-confidence. Our soul is God's pure presence, God's unique expression, God's peace inside of us. Each of us has our own experience of perfect being, which then extends outward through our personality and our life in the world.

The perfection we experience is real security. It gives an identity of being-ness instead of what roles and activities we are attached to. Immortality is our true nature. The experience of the soul includes this feeling that everything is present. Nothing is denied. The separation is over.

> *Everything is profoundly present. No need to wish for anything. Our thoughts come from our well of being, immense being.*

With soft, open hands we are experiencing life as if being carried. God is seen and felt as permeating all beings, all things, everything before us and in us. No matter how limited or separate we may be, this fullness, this thickness of God permeates completely. Everything that is solid in the world or seemingly fixed in our minds is really moving, liquid God.

In this awareness, the demands of the normal world are very far away. Within our no self, our soul unfolds. Our awareness finds food, real nurturing every time we take the opportunity to go and be inside. This presence is very full and expanding, spreading beyond our bodies, beyond the room we are in. We keep expanding until we feel our presence as large as the planet and still spreading to the stars. This is in everyone. It is the awareness of our soul. It is the awareness of the great masters. They stand in their infinite ground of being. As our soul unfolds, we have moments and sometimes longer experiencing the knowing. We stand in the part of us that is a great Master, saint, or mystic living in our ground of being, our soul.

When we return to our normal personality, daily world, life as we usually know it is different, changed. The experiences we have inside are still with us. To know our soul does not deny the existence of our personality or our worldly self. But now, our thoughts and feelings struggle less.

> *Our personality is nurtured directly from our soul. We remember our true security, comfort, innocence, source of life and creativity.*

Instead of growing a complicated life of unnecessary drama, the soul reminds us of the beauty of simplicity, love, service in all relationships and activities. Our soul naturally unfolds into a life of joy. Life is planned less and lived more. Our soul unfolds in and through our world until we let go into eternity.

## At Home in Both Worlds

Some people are afraid that being open to these experiences will make them weak and ineffective in their daily life. Our knowing our inner well of being, does not take anything away from our effectiveness in the world. It only changes our priorities. We find less reason to struggle or search for something, which is already inside of us. Our truth makes us self-confident. We can be available for joy and still be clear with one another. Our inner self is as much personal power as it is a vast landscape of simple awareness.

In the modern world, the energy of fear and competition makes it difficult to soften our hearts, feel the joy, and open to other parts of ourselves. This is why we need our own place like an altar in our homes. We need to make time for a daily spiritual practice or retreat. Our hearts deserve space and time where we can feel safe to let go of our worldly self and explore inside. Our life of joy naturally includes a world of spiritual beings.

> *Protective Angels and other Divine beings shelter us. No matter how much the modern world denies spirituality, the denial does not make it so.*

Children and older people naturally feel the protective presence and the reality of their souls. Those who have explored their hearts naturally feel their soul unfolding from within. Angels, divine beings, realms of lightness of being are with us as we open to our essence. The pure love of our soul is at the same frequency, vibration. In our expanded being there is much presence. God is not separate from us as many people think. In the life of our soul each aspect of God is a part of us. God is our ground of being, our inner garden from where we abundantly, fearlessly create, live, and give.

We have the opportunity to feel everything human, the beauty of this life, and our daily world deeply in our hearts. We can enjoy and be not afraid because the soul is the experience of our no self in eternity. Our soul offers us seemingly a separate reality, a world of its own. We can be in this world and simultaneously be in a completely new awareness. In the empty space of no thought an ever-expanding experience opens. Without identity there is nothing to protect, nothing to fear, nothing. Everything is very light. This reality is a world without grasping; it is an unloading, where all awareness in our heart gets lighter and lighter, softer and softer as if coming back to our origin. We somehow intimately know this original awareness inside of us.

This experience is not a fantasy. It is not some mental realm we create but unfolds naturally in our awareness when we are in the seat of our joy, our soul. Many people have theses experience in dreams and meditation but chose not to discuss them. In the life of joy, it is important to give words to our experience. We are called to speak out as spiritual beings if a balance is to be returned to modern culture. There is more to life then the physical and mental world that keeps us busy.

Our normal worldly concerns are temporary. They are like clouds. Ultimately, they do not exist. The sky is clear and unlimited. This awareness is like a pure bath washing away every heaviness and seriousness of daily life. We look further inside to our ground of being. Some people literally experience their ground of being or the body of their soul as an ocean. It is an ocean of water, ocean of flowers or flower petals. Others experience the inner Earth as soil full of lightness, very peaceful. The soil goes deeper and deeper inside like the depths of the Earth. Some people experience their ground of being as just endless being, accepting, and warm. The experience is like dissolving into finer and finer qualities of awareness. Some people experience their ground as literally a fire, a great fire totally freeing, and peaceful. The ground of being can be a realm full of light, Buddha, Mary, or Christ. God is the ground of being, the body and essence of their soul. To touch the ground of being in whatever form is to find nectar, a sweet honey, which is the essence of creation inside. The ground evolves as the heart is breathed into, expanded, and lived.

Our experience changes as we offer and receive our source of pure being. We can simply be, drinking the nectar of the discoveries we make inside. Our ground, our soul is not something we earn or accomplish. The separation from our mind to our hearts and from our hearts and to our soul is something we each have created. We can find our way back home. In our depths we feel the nurturing of our source.

*God seems to originate, uniquely within us and extends in us and through us to the world and the stars. Enlightenment is an awareness of joy's abundance.*

Light permeates the world and everything in it. How can we be this awareness all the time? The life of our soul is running into the arms of God again and again. It is our calling to joy!

# Human Versus Divine, Good Versus Evil

In the unfolding of our soul we enjoy all the realms of being human and divine. Many of us are fighting with our selves trying to achieve some spiritual supremacy. Our human nature often seems in the way. Some of us give up and are depressed with the judgments that we have placed on our selves and our spiritual life. Joy's calling teaches us there is no competition. Our Divine experience comes from the acceptance of our most human self. Our inner peace grows as our interior life is explored and embraced.

> *We learn to celebrate our human nature as the soil from which our divine awareness grows. When we hold our smallest self as if it is also God, the life of our soul is truly present and growing.*

## Our Human Divinity

On joy's path, we can eat and drink, party and joke. Then a few minutes later we may close our eyes and travel into heavenly realms or sit with someone and feel the far reaches of their soul. There is no contradiction, no inner struggle trying to be holy by denying being human. We know ourselves, our human divinity. Our human weaknesses live right next to our divine self. People in pain see angels. Others in personal conflict feel suddenly great light around them or within them. We never know when our awareness is suddenly in another dimension, a dimension of no self, unlimited being. The human and divine worlds are parallel to each other, independent of one another and at times overlapping. There are times to purposely set aside to be in the heart's great quietude. And there are times of activity which maybe just as purposeful. This is life's mystery. The small self can be very present and we can have an awareness of an ocean of light in the midst of feeling very small and insignificant. There are different worlds, different drummers, different rules. Joy is the path, the bridge, the beginning and end. Joy is the air all life has in common. The world is divine and it is full of separation and suffering. Intellectually we can understand but only in our hearts do we overcome the separation, our own difficulty that keeps us separate.

In the journey, we can find place for both our human desires and divine experience. They are not exclusive. There are many rooms in the heart. Daily joys, spiritual joys, sexual bliss and bliss of great peace all come from the same heart. When the heart is not in conflict with itself, many rooms open.

### Good and Evil

When we enter the worlds beyond our normal self, we may begin to wonder about the presence of good and evil. Does evil really exist or is it just my fear? Does good overcome evil or is this only my acceptance of my lower self? Is there good and evil beyond my own process? How do we know what ultimately exists?

Depending upon the culture, good and evil are related to in different ways. In the West, with our strong belief in good and that goodness eventually prevails, we live in this understanding of the goodness of life while sending forgiveness, compassion, understanding, and truth to the forces of evil. These forces are found within our own psyche and in the world around us.

In some parts of the East, good and evil are seen as equal parts of life. The bad characters in religious theater and stories are not destroyed but managed and allowed to live for another day. To chase after good and battle with evil only invites more chasing and future battles for us in our lives. To acknowledge the presence of good and evil in life gives more space to creative living and transformation. Personally and globally, good and evil are present. They are equal parts of the world we live in. Life is light and dark, good and evil.

In other parts of the East, neither good nor evil are ultimately real. Good and evil are seen as part of the divine play. Everyone understands that each part of the play has consequences. Each are here to learn to choose carefully when and how in the play they show up. They do not want to disturb the theatre of the Gods but choose to meet in the place where all the Gods have found their liberation.

In every culture, the mystic is committed to life and this includes playing the role of truth in daily live. When the mystic closes his eyes, he sees clearly what is happening inside of him. When the mystic opens his eyes, he sees just as clearly what is happening around him.

> *When we learn to breathe every part of our life, and everyone in our life in and out of our heart, we help heal the great separation.*

We discover ourselves in God's ocean. Living from our ground of being frees us from the acting and reacting to the events around us. From our ground of being, we find our life energy for serving. Living close to our ground of being, we can appear and disappear in the dramas around us, as we want to. Our ground of being is much greater than any evil because our ground of being is God in all the cosmos. As we are grounded in our true being, good and evil, the dualism, no longer exist. We have many choices how to be, serve, and enjoy. Our own truth is our guide, shelter, and source.

## *An Opening In The Heart*

In our intention for the Divine, the Divine unfolds inside of us. People of diverse backgrounds and religion express similar experiences of the soul as in the following description; "One day when meditating I noticed a small opening inside my heart. Through the small hole I saw an incredible, very bright white, clear light. The opening was quite small but as my awareness drew closer, the light was very bright. I could hardly look into it. It seemed this space was like a sliver in my heart. Or was it the heart of Christ? I did not know. But when I looked into it, I was totally transformed. There was no space for doubt, need, or desire. Everything was present. When my awareness returned to one side, I became aware of only my normal self. Then when I looked through the opening, this light was so true that anything I thought immediately found its truth. Whatever I imagined, wished, or saw was present. The light was so perfect, that I was aware of only how balanced and perfect I am, everything is. In this light there was no lacking, nothing missing. Everything was present, complete. When I was back in my normal awareness I sensed all my normal problems and challenges. When I returned to peeking into the light, my problems or difficulties were dissolved. Everything was healed, whole, just by the intensity, the purity of the light. I offered myself to this light. I received the light. At times I was in it and other times it was all around me. Then I found myself in my normal awareness again. This process continued for some days. With my whole being I wanted to become an instrument of this light, this perfection. Coming from being in this light, my human awareness was so heavy. Life's difficulties seemed true when I stood outside the light. But I knew they were not true. In the light, there was no separation. The light held everything, all answers, all solutions, all fulfillments. It simply was. Meanwhile, in contrast, my normal awareness was so separate, missing an anchor in the light. This must be why we so often do not know what to do, where to turn, how to manage. We are so separate from the absolute inside of us, our perfect light. The truth is so brilliant, so bright, so overwhelmingly present."

These experiences come in many forms but with similar intensity and life changing truth. These experiences often stay with us for years. To remember these experiences is to be supported again and again in joy's path. Slowly our identity takes root inside these openings in the heart. As the opening grows larger, our soul unfolds in our life.

# Death, No Death

In the modern world, we live as if there is no death. Then when someone does die, we live as if there is complete death. We behave as if the person is fully gone and forever separate from us and those who loved him or her. No one thinks much about death until it comes. Then when there is death, there is finality. We live daily as if there is no death and then when someone close to us dies, there is only death, the end.

The truth, of course, is exactly the opposite. There is death. There will be the death of our body and worldly self. Death is always present. It can come at anytime. Then the world as we regularly know it, is gone. After we leave our body, we realize there is no death. Our awareness goes on. We are not as separate as we imagined from family and love ones. The essence that bonds us is real. We are still bonded. Many people have experiences of loved ones who had died who come to visit them. They come into their dreams. The dreams are so real they are surprised to wake up and see it was a dream. They come into their thoughts so vividly that they do not believe it is only their thoughts. We are again together. Departed ones often come into the room. Their presence is so real and certainly is not our imagination. Departed love ones visit and confirm their new life all the time. In modern culture there is no support to talk about these experiences, so many people simply enjoy the confirmation and the love and do not speak about it.

In the modern world dying for many, is a painfully slow process of letting go. As we get older we let go again and again of friends and loved ones. One-step after another we are letting go of our bodies and the activities, which were routine until recently. In modern culture because of our separation from God and eternity, dying is very difficult, fearful, and lonely. On the path of joy it is exactly the opposite. Instead of being fearful and lonely, we are remembering real food, the joy that is still with us. We are remembering God, our ground of pure being. The presence of loved ones already departed are felt close by. Less activity in the world is more joy experienced inside. We are resting more. Letting go is also a going inside. Our vast, soft, inner being awaits us. We discover more and more inside. A pure presence is growing within us. Joy is leading us from the activity of the world to a new activity. We are surrendering and moving into our home in the heart. There is so much peace to receive.

## Cherishing the Gifts of Life

Learning to die is learning to live fully. We are aware of the preciousness of life including the gift of our bodies, personalities, family, and friends. Our joy does not allow us to take for granted the gifts of life around us. Each day we want to enjoy the many moments. We want to receive this life fully. To be a soul in a body, to see, hear, touch, feel life through the heart, this is a continuous wonder. Joy has healed much of our separation from life, others, and ourselves. In this healing of separation, joy has made a bridge between every day life and eternity. Joy is the common essence in both worlds. In our hearts, we understand the uniqueness and value of our lives while we already feel the presence of eternity. Each day is full of so many simple moments of beauty. Life is sacred.

In the ending period of our lives are opportunities of great heartfulness and understanding. We are being prepared for the great compassion, forgiveness, and wisdom of the other side. We understand when we leave our bodies, no one is there asking how much money we made or how big a house we lived in. There is no one asking what we did or did not do in this life. There is no one asking even how we behaved or didn't behave. There is only a question of love. How much love did we open to? How much joy did we deny others and ourselves?

## Experiences in Dying

Beliefs in many cultures and reports from people who have technically died but later revived report many similarities. When we leave our bodies, our problems, normal concerns, and time disappear. At first we find ourselves hovering over our body. Before we have time to worry about what or how to proceed, there is a fast vibration taking us. Our soul has departed our body and is being lifted immediately to its own vibration. We are traveling through a tunnel into the dimension of unlimited space, a bright light, intense light of joy. In this tunnel, sometimes just before or after the tunnel, we see loved ones and friends we know who already have left their bodies. We meet our heart of hearts, our Lord or we may meet simple pure Light. This light is also mysteriously a part of us. It is we. We are remembering. Our soul resonates in a "yes". Our soul is breathing as if having a new breath for the first time in a long time. There is so much "yes" to remember. Meanwhile another part of us recoils in the bright light as if saying "yes, but". Then in this moment we see a review of our lives, thousands of moments pass through us. There is no time. We do not know if this review is within seconds, hours, or days. We are just witnessing thousands of moments of love received and love turned away. We see every part of us that is not of this joyful light. In this moment we see the "yes" and the "yes but" in response to this dimension of very bright light.

Most of us start grasping, looking for our physical reality, and the story we knew. We begin reaching for the mental and emotional being we were accustomed to. In this grasping we resonate to realms of being closer to this physical world. We find ourselves neither in our normal world nor in the great light. We may see Heaven or sense it in the distance, but we cannot seem to arrive there. Other beings are around, consoling us, helping us. Some of us think we must be in Heaven because we are aware that life continues. It is only life of another sort that we find continuing. We may not know quite what is happening and we may reincarnate almost directly back into a body. Still others of us whose consciousness is full of dark and violent deeds quickly find ourselves in darker realms.

*There are many realms between our realities on Earth and the realities of Heaven. Depending upon our life of joy, the life of our soul, we resonate to one of these realms.*

Those of us who more or less know only our physical being resonate to a more physical reality or reincarnate quickly. Others who know life mostly as a mental or emotional experience find themselves in realms of similar mental and emotional energy. Yet we cannot judge. Some people who live a very physical life may find themselves waking up upon death to the full life and joy of their soul. They may awaken easily and arrive into great realms of light. Others who seemingly lived through dark times full of emotional difficulty may also quickly awaken and find themselves carried by angels into great spheres of being. We cannot judge others or ourselves. Parts of our soul may be hidden from others or ourselves so that we can live a particular path in Earthly life. Once released from our bodies, these hidden realms inside of us awaken and we continue our journey into eternity.

Usually, however, the life of joy resonates quickly to Heavenly joys when we leave our bodies. When we know joy, love's pure joy, we resonate to this vast space and feel "yes". Our "yes" takes us further and further into joyful realms. We are not grasping but unfolding. We are not pulled back but expanding. Joy is our liberation, our fire, and our light expanding to more pure essence. We travel in simple thought. There are realms so complete that before even thought we are here. Our physical body has let go to our mental and emotional body that has surrendered to joy's body. Joy's body has let go to our essence.

Here there is not a thread of personality remaining held together. We find ourselves just expanding awareness, joining, being our unlimited being. From our hearts, we have received, unfolded, let go, and become free. We have come home.

> *Some of us continue unfolding, unfolding until even the body of our awareness has let go into the universe of sweetness. We dissolve back completely into God.*

We may join gardens and wonder full Heavenly stories. We may continue to have a body of awareness. We continue the life of joy just in much lighter, more peaceful circumstances. It is hard to find words to explain such other worldly experiences. The realms of joy we know in this life are the closest experience we can have to the life in eternity.

Those of us who identify with only our personal story find our awareness grasping for new story, physical and emotional life, as we knew it. Those of us who strongly identify with pictures find our awareness grasping for new pictures to manage our new experience. When we know our ground of being, we find ourselves letting go into eternity's vast ground of pure being.

Joy's calling is our preparation for eternity. Joy heals many of our separations. Our ground of being heals much of our fear of death. Our awareness knows the presence of eternity, whose denial is the root of much suffering. The joy in this moment is the same joy in eternity. Now and when we leave our bodies, we either grasp outside for control and identity or surrender and feel the journey inside unfolding. Our souls continue unfolding. Reaching and experiencing the greatest light, the greatest joy, helps free our soul into vast realms.

The bridge to joy in this world is not so different to the bridges in the realms beyond us. Love helps us to pass easily. From our inner heart, our essence is unfolding. This is the opposite of self-importance, trying to manage and do something. In the spirit of forgiveness, we sail through space. Trying to control or accomplish, in this space, only makes our awareness become heavier and more difficult. The vibration of joy, the soft golden heart, the ground of our true being is expanding. We sense our selves spreading further and further. We are not going into Heaven as much as we are letting go into our own pure being. Inside or outside, we are our no self. We are vast being. It is as if we are carried. Life is less from our own effort and more an experience of being given, grace. Beings seen and unseen, divine presence known and unknown are carrying us. They are with us and in us. They are we.

We realize the separations we feel between God and us are only our imaginings. We are not separate. Joy's path has been healing this perception through our remembering. Joy's calling has been bringing us to union, to awareness that God and everything good is not outside of us, not separate from us. God is everything. We are surrounded in God. As we remember our essence, this essence is found to be universal. The greatest realms inside of us are now everywhere as we leave the heaviness and separateness of this physical reality.

Death brings us to the awareness there is no death. This is why it is important to pray for our dear ones, who have recently left their bodies. Holding their essence in our hearts helps their awareness adjust; to death and that there is no death. The separation lets go to receiving each other in our thoughts and dreams, our hearts and simple being. Feeling the essence of family members and friends with us, affirms the life of our souls in everyone. Receiving one another, our soul continues unfolding. The great separation around death in modern culture calls for our joy. Joy heals the fear and loneliness. Joy opens the doors to eternity now until we realize there is no death.

# Becoming an Instrument

We are each called to become instruments of peace and joy. In the unfolding of our soul, this is natural. As we find our joy, we become more and more our true selves. Our body, our life is our instrument. Most of us have instruments playing a noisy song of compromise, self-sacrifice, and struggle. Real food nurtures the pure sound within us. The calling of joy is remembering our essence that is felt in our hearts and then expressed in the world. In our practice of accepting emptiness, the noise and fear of the daily world is set free. Here is real peace for us to feel and receive. Here is the peace the world hungers for. When we project our ground into our relationships and work, we have more expectations and less peace for ourselves and others.

*Our ground of being is our true source of peace. From here we listen, create, and spread our essence, through our hearts, out into the world.*

We become intimate with our instrument. Our body, personality, our no self form a perfect instrument. As we offer everything in our hearts and receive our true being, our sound is clearer and clearer. Our instrument, our song, our path is ours, unique.

*Rediscovering our own sound is sacred.*

In the life of our soul, how do we know what to choose? Do we to take the road into nature or visit with family and friends in the city? How do we know if we should work in a large company or alone, solely? How do we know the life we are called to? Joy's being seems to be almost everywhere when our hearts are present. How do we know what is for our highest good and greatest service, or our life's fullest purpose?

St. Francis of Assisi, over eight hundred years ago, answered this question for us. Through his prayer to become an instrument of peace, we find the course of our soul. As we are our well of being, finely tuned in our passion and truth, our sound is whole. We are whole. We play our joy. When we become instruments, we live our true path. As most people adjust to the noise around them and compromise their joy, we, as instruments, set an example for others to become their own instrument of joy.

## Listening to Our Joy's Yearning

The quality of our sound directly depends upon the qualities of our soul that we are remembering. Our decisions are a result of our listening to our soul's yearning and our maturing wisdom. We know what choices to make each day because we feel what is right for us in our bodies. Our instrument knows to decide whether to be in nature today or whether to into the city. Our instrument, our whole being just knows. As we get more and more tuned to what is true for us, we know which way is true and which way is not. As we listen and express our joy, our instrument plays and plays what is natural and true for us. It sounds right. It feels right. People recognize we are being true to ourselves. When we make a wrong choice this sounds and feels wrong. We are out of tune. Our instrument may be different and misunderstood by others, but for us it is perfect. It is our truth, our essence, our intentions that are unfolding.

Each of us has different gifts, which are our instrument to receive, appreciate, and offer in the world. Someone for example, a teacher or writer, may express their heart through their heart felt words. Someone may offer dance, music, or art. Someone may garden, cook, or make crafts. Others may design, offer counseling or guidance. Any creativity that comes from the heart is our talent to open to and unfold our soul into the world. Many people find their talent but limit the creative experience being more concerned with what others may think or want. The soul gets compromised, sold out, abandoned because of our fears and inability to open to our depths of joy. Many of us have opened our gift, we know our instrument, but our souls compete with our worries and concerns. Most creativity does not find its true sound, express its true instrument because the soul is not given space to unfold. We are not prepared with real food, emptiness, letting go of our pictures and our personal story. We do not know our ground of being. Our instrument is used for entertainment, making money, to impress others, many things but to unfold our soul into our lives.

Becoming an instrument relaxes our minds about what we should do and say, what our life should look like in the world. We are finding the pure sound inside. As we live from our ocean of being, we naturally express it in the world through our particular talent, our instrument.

# *Silence*

In silence we hear the perfect sound of our instrument. We can never have too much silence.

> *The loss of silence in the modern world is threatening to the world of joy because in the silence, joy finds its full expression.*

In silence we can hear the true voice inside of us. We can relax in the peace of silence. As many people are busy trying to fill the silence with activity or noise, our instrument calls us to be empty, empty to the riches hidden in the silence. The silence we find in the world, helps us to find the silence within us. Our soul can breathe and expand. In the silence we remember our depths of being. The silence heals the complicated life. Silence washes the noise, in and around us away. Silence releases our awareness from being so tightly wrapped in and around our personal story. Silence embraces our emptiness. It fills the nothing inside with the sweetness of simple being. Silence restores us. Our passion, intuition, and creativity find their source again. In the silence our no self is clear. We are our source in the silence. We are available in worlds of Divine presence. Silence and our soul's joy are one and the same.

> *Finding the silence within us, we begin to find the silence in every relationship, the silence in every conversation, the silence underneath our words, and in every activity.*

Silence heals our separation. The silence we find in those around us, in nature, in every part of life, keeps us close to our essence, our heart of hearts, and our joyful nature. As one culture can have dozens of words for snow, the mystic has as many words for silence. Silence can be sacred, simple, pure, natural, open, humble, peaceful, other worldly, truthful, empty, strong, light, delicate, clear, honey, vulnerable, creative, healing, gentle, relaxing, giving, receiving, offering, graceful, holy, anything but ordinary. These are the notes of our soul unfolding, the notes of our instrument. Silence is always fresh, alive, new. Silence is perfect food, nurturing every nerve of our being, giving pure joy. In the unfolding of our soul we can never have too much silence. Silence opens doors in the life of our soul without effort. Silence is the great shelter for everything good to unfold within us and come to us.

# The Gift of the Little Flowers

Looking to life as a gift keeps us in the realms of our lightness of being. The gift of this moment keeps our awareness expanding, serving, and being. Life's grace and bliss are never far away. Many of us are quick to put each other into categories of better or worse, friend or foe. In general, we are too busy to receive the gift each person brings to us. Joy calls us to receive the best of everyone, each experience. The calling is to receive the best of life from moment to moment. From our ground of being, we are letting go of everything else. Life is a gift leading to our natural abundance.

As we understand the gift, we have an experience of every moment being lifted, every person, every occasion being lifted to its highest possibility. This lifting life up is not an obligation or duty. It simply is.

> *When we receive life as a gift we are naturally lifting the moment to its beauty, life's potentiality. We are lifting the moment to its finest qualities.*

The practice of gratitude is the most direct path of unfolding our soul in our life. In our gratitude our soul flourishes, meadows of colorful joy are surfacing in our hearts and in our lives.

> *There is a space between our desires and our worries. This space is our ground of being. It is here that life's little flowers grow and blossom.*

Our soul unfolds here. Again and again through the heart, we receive life's garden.

Our soul calls us to an intimate relationship with life itself. The little flowers come expectedly or unexpectedly from any direction and most important from inside of us. The simple heart allows us to go further inside to the inner reaches, the starry universe of our soul. Inexplicably we are home in all the vast worlds within and beyond us. Here we find fields and fields of flowers. Inside our soul we breathe into meadows and meadows of wild flowers. Each blossom is a world of peace to inhale and receive. The little flowers found inside awaken us to the little flowers in everyday life. Golden moments are available every moment we remember God, our soul's presence, as we stand in our ground of being. The little flowers are perfect food. They are our soul. This is the path of the little flowers. Our souls are unfolding into millions of golden moments. Joy is dancing through our being; it is dancing in the blossoms at our feet with the stars over our heads. Our creativity, the choices we make, the people we live with, are all inspired by joy's presence. The little flowers know no end in their beauty. The little flowers carry us. Each one is full of the essence of joy. They carry us into our life in eternity.

Little flowers eat when they are hungry. They sleep when they are tired. They don't think too much or do too much. Little flowers are busy being. There is so much life inside and outside. Little flowers don't argue with life. They enjoy. The life of a little flower is quite simple. Indeed, the life of the little flowers is quite natural. Our innocence is found again and again in our ground of being. In our innocence the questions in life about what to think, what to do, what to eat and wear become quite simple. The life of the little flowers is joy's calling.

# Beginner's Mind

Joy grows as we practice beginners mind. Each time we offer everything we are carrying inside, we are new again. We have beginner's mind. When we remember our hearts then our thoughts are connected to our ground of being and we are not just busy. The life we are creating becomes our awareness growing and expanding in this moment. Beginner's mind frees us. We are letting go of unnecessary attachments, preoccupation, and entanglements.

> *Our personal story is only the clothing we are wearing. Beginner's mind reminds us, we are our well of being.*

Each time we think we already know, each time we jump ahead in our thoughts to what is happening or what will be, we deny the current of joy in this moment finding its own way. Each person during the day, we meet as if for the first time, even if we have known them for years. Each day at work is new, for the first time, even if we have done the same work for seemingly forever. Having beginners mind keeps us in the present, open, soft, and available for the mandala of life's mystery.

## For the First Time

The ordinary things, the routine activities all have potential for mystical beauty when we have beginner's mind. We are seeing, hearing, and sensing life for the first time. This day is entirely new. With beginners mind we are giving others, circumstances, and life, space to change and grow. Indeed this moment is new. Beginners mind frees us from old judgments or criticisms that limit our thoughts to what we have known. Beginners mind keeps life fresh and alive. In our knowing is

215

the profound reality of our unknowing. It is all right not to know and to discover instead. In our innocence, life is beginning again and again. An old friend or lifelong partner is seen with new eyes, new heart. Who is this person who I thought I already knew so well? With beginners mind, someone new is sitting with us. The most ordinary activity is experienced differently as we give close attention to the details and our experience of the moment. Every time we remember, our true self, our no self, we are experiencing beginner's mind.

When we enter the moment with beginners mind, we are in God's presence and life's infinite possibilities. Our soul is unfolding through us and into the world.

# Appendix: Practical Spirituality

# *Appendix 1:*
## *Ten Simple Steps to Joy*

1.  Sit and reflect on memories of Joy. Go back as far as you can, when you were three, five, eight, twelve, or fifteen. Recover your memories of joy. Sit with them. Let these memories of joy nourish your being now. Let these memories inspire you to new joys today. Inside every adult is a child ready to play. Let your past joys inspire you to what would be joy for you today.

2.  If life is overwhelming in stress and joy seems very away or if joy is present and life is good, practice the offering. For five or ten minutes each day try to let go of all your stress or joy. Let go of everything you are holding in your awareness. Practice being present. For a few minutes everyday give your self a rest. Let go of everything and everyone you are carrying in your heart. The crowded heart cannot find joy. This letting go can be while simply sitting, taking a bath, or walking in nature. Give your heart the gift to feel it self. Joy will find a way when there is some space. Being complete present allows the past to fall away and the future to find a new beginning. Complete offering opens us to deep receiving.

3.  If you are worrying a lot and joy just does not have a reality to you, take some time and have the intention to make friends with the fear underneath your worries about health, money, a close relative or friend. Hold your heart and the fears inside, as if you were holding a small child. Embrace your inner child. Do something fun today! Be gentle with yourself. Listen, accept, make friends with this empty place inside where fear

and worries are busy. Joy comes when we make an act of love towards our self.

4.  If you do not know where to begin in finding real food, practice having one simple joy each day. One day this may be having a coffee in an outside café. The next day it may be calling an old friend. Then the next it may be taking the time to walk through a beautiful park. Find joy one day at a time. Make a practice of real food, one experience at a time.

5.  Give yourself the joy of silence. For a period every day turn off all the machines in your house. Turn off everything so your heart and soul can feel themselves. Give your self the joy of silence. Silence feeds every nerve in your body with its pure presence. The soul can unfold and find a home in this quiet.

6.  Love your body. The body is the home of the soul. Until we leave this home, loving your body may be an important step to loving ourselves more deeply and finding our joy. Often those who treat their bodies poorly, treat their souls in a similar manner. Love your body.

7.  Seek friends and community that understand joy. Life is more than being busy, practical, and serious. Seek friends and community who are finding real food, and joy in a way that means something to you. Your soul will help guide you. Hold the intention of true friends and community. One friend who you can share what is in your heart is as great as any treasure this world can offer.

8.  Service almost always frees us from being preoccupied with ourselves to see life in a new way. Service is not what we do with our money as much as giving our hands and heart to someone else to make their journey a little easier. Service frees us from our selves to a bigger self that includes another.

9.  If life was a gift, what part of the gift is most important for you now? Imagine receiving this gift. Perhaps it is love, abundance, health. Practice receiving the gift that you yearn for. Feel the substance of this experience with you now. In this yearning is your soul. Allow yourself to feel this yearning deeply. You soul is not so far away. And when you soul is not so far away, joy is always near by.

10. Joy. Every evening take a few minutes and sit with the truest moment of the day. This is your joy! Remember as many of the details you can. Be with the experience again as if it is happening now. Feel the joy in every part of your heart. Receive the joy in your whole being. Remembering joy is to remember a greater part of ourselves, our soul. Joy is pure food.

# Appendix 2:
# Meditations for Joy

Practice each meditation for seven days. Then repeat the practice of each meditation for another seven days. If one particular meditation speaks to you now begin there. Save the other meditations for later. The important thing is to not be too busy and take sometime to grow our inner life, our joy. Take time and make space for meditations of joy.

## Simple Sitting

Take thirty minutes each day. Preferably the same time each day. Simply sit. Do not worry. The mind may wander. Thoughts may keep coming about the day and plans. Simply sit. Taking these thirty minutes daily is a reminder to step out of the busy life, work, and relationships that have a hold on our being. These thirty minutes are an opportunity to loosen the mental stress tying us up in our daily world. It is our opportunity to let go. Stepping out of our personal story, the best we can, sitting each day for thirty minutes allows joy to find space inside. No matter what the challenges of our story may present, sitting is slowing down, giving room for new possibilities, greater being. We are giving ourselves back to ourselves. The daily world slowly has some distance and we can feel our self, our seat of joy!

## Offering and Receiving

Begin the meditation by offering, letting go of everything our awareness is conscious of carrying in our hearts. Thoughts, feelings, concerns, hope, all of our awareness is offered. Slowly we find more peace inside. We want to rest in this peace. We want to receive this inner peace. Then we offer again. Take several minutes offering again all that we are aware of carrying in our hearts. Gradually the breath out can be as a release, letting go of all that we are carrying. The breath inside is resting in our peace. Offering and receiving, we are slowly carrying less of the world inside of us and feeling more of our own river of being. Offering and receiving, soon our river opens to the ocean of our being.

## Meditation on God's presence

God is not an idea. God is not a feeling. The experience of God's presence begins with the experience of our own energy. God is not separate from us. Sit and feel your own presence. Thoughts come and go. This is your time to simply be and experience your own energy. As you experience your own essence, receive the peace. This peace is the beginning of God inside of you. Practice heartfulness, understanding, compassion, and forgiveness with yourself and with everything you find inside. God is in the small stream, large river, seas and ocean of heartfulness, understanding, compassion, and forgiveness you find inside. God is. Slowly you are more and more simple presence. This is the growth of joy, God inside of you.

## Meditation on nakedness

For some people, the mind is just too busy to allow the experience of some simple peace. A good meditation for humbling the mind to the fullness of the soul is to meditate on one's nakedness. Nakedness begins with our physical being. No matter how much comfort we have, how nice our clothes, belongings, friends, work, and life maybe, we are still profoundly naked. Life can change any moment. No matter how much security we think we have, there is no security. We are truly naked. The weather can change, work can change, relationships can change, life can take an entire new course or end at any moment. We are naked, vulnerable. Simply sit and feel your vulnerability. This is nakedness. We are vulnerable no matter how much or important we think we are. This meditation is about making friends, listening to, being with, and holding our vulnerability. Vulnerability, nakedness is not our enemy. As human beings we are vulnerable. We are naked. This is not a time to let the mind wander into all our fearful fantasies of what could happen to us. Be in the moment. Hold your heart. Acknowledge how naked this moment is. To simply be in the moment is to be vulnerable. Taking time to feel our nakedness everyday can change how we view ourselves, others, the decisions we make, what we hold as important. Nakedness can remind us not to take the opinions of others, our duties, and responsibilities so seriously. We are naked. Everyone is naked. Joy can now breathe new life in the fresh awareness of our nakedness.

## Heart Meditation, Golden Self

Everyday simply sit with whatever is in your heart. Maybe you go inside your heart and feel a loved one, a teacher, God. Maybe you go inside and feel frustration, desire, attachment to someone or events going your way. Ok! Simply take the time to sit with your heart. Practice accepting, being with whatever you find in your heart. The small self, true self, no self, each day love who you find. In your heart is the purity of being, your golden essence, your natural peace. Even if you do not experience this right away, it is still there. Have heartfulness, understanding, compassion, forgiveness for everything you find in your heart. Sit and receive your heart. This is your home of joy! Joy begins here. Taking the time to sit with our hearts, we are taking the time to know ourselves.

Slowly we find new rooms inside. There is much more to who we are. There are worlds and worlds inside our heart waiting for our exploration. There is a great space, immense light, guidance, joy, our golden self to receive. There is our golden being to offer and receive in every corner of our heart. This gold is pure food, the real treasure to open and enjoy.

## Meditation on eternity

All of life's details fill our awareness. It is important to take the time to meditate on eternity, our life beyond the details that keep us busy. Meditation on eternity is not thinking about the idea of eternity as how we might imagine. It is a specific experience. The experience of eternity begins within our hearts. We go inside. We feel softness or a space of being. We go deeper inside. The softness increases or the space widens. We breathe and let go further inside. There is more and more space. Do not be distracted by thoughts. They go by. Do not be tempted to let you mind be caught up with creative ideas or visions. Relax and be as deeply within yourself. Breathe and let go. The breath in takes you to an ocean of being. The breath out lets go into an ocean of being. This is your time to be with your ocean of being. Receive your image of God in these moments or simply receive the pure being of your heart.

Do not control your experience. Let the energy expand. Let the experience find its own course. There is no right or wrong. Again, there is no right or wrong. If you find something unpleasant do not be afraid. Offer it love and stay with your pure presence of being. Letting go of any struggle, any fear. The experience will change. Simply being in the reservoir of no self.

Some days its may be easy to go inside and be with your true self, eternity. Other days you might find everything but your expansive self. Heartfulness, understanding, compassion, forgiveness are your tools for meditation. Take the time for the experience of eternity. It is here. It is inside of you. Eternity grows inside as your awareness receives its presence. The experience of eternity grows inside as you take time for eternity.

## Meditation for Negativity

Once the vast space inside is found, we have a new resource to transform the negativity we find with ourselves and in the world. Sitting in our vast inner space, we breathe in our negativity and/or the negativity we find in the world and exhale our love. The vast space inside is greater then any darkness, fear, or negativity we can find or imagine. The vast space inside is without limit. God is always greater! This meditation is a practice of knowing the unlimited body of joy. Breathing in negativity can transform ourselves, others, any situation. But the goal is not to change the situation other then to find harmony. I inhale all darkness into the vast being and exhale into the vast being. I inhale all negativity into the vast being and exhale into the vast being. I inhale and exhale in and out of the vast, unlimited being.

## Meditation of The Little Flowers

Each day, there are the little flowers of love's presence. This meditation is a reminder to receive the gifts of the little flowers deeper in our hearts. Today's flowers may be a special moment with a family member or friend, the crisp air at sunrise, remembering a feeling or bright color in a dream. The little flowers of Divine presence come in many forms. This meditation is to take the time and receive these moments more fully, letting the experience be more thoroughly in our awareness and hearts. Life's garden manifests one flower at a time. Each little flower opens the door inside to God's beauty and simple love.

## Earth Meditation

Sit and find the large space inside. In this space you can visualize the planet earth surrounded in an atmosphere of golden, warm light. As if the Earth is your small baby, hold the Earth and let your love resonate all around it and through it. For fifteen minutes or longer, let the Earth be cradled in your heart and arms, as your awareness becomes this vast space of love embracing all life on the planet.

Now begin the meditations over again. Practice each meditation for a week or as long as it is still nourishing you.

# *Appendix 3:*
# *Joy Support Groups*

A group that meets regularly to support each other to find real food to unfold their souls can have many benefits. Each person has the opportunity to explore and discuss what real food means and what is their unique experience of living a life of their soul. The group environment is a shelter for remembering, rediscovering, and making new steps. The open sharing of how each experiences their joy and their soul unfolding is a big support to bring our inner life out into the open and make it okay. Joy support groups make it okay to be vulnerable, empty, be light full, to enjoy ecstasy, and find our own truth and experience of God.

1. Meet regularly for example the same time every week or every other week.

2. Begin with a half hour meditation; perhaps use a meditation from above to begin.

3. Give each person time to talk about their private life and the real food they have experienced since the last meeting. During the personal sharing it is important that the others do not react, no preaching, no teaching. Everyone is simply listening.

4. Take turns being Group leader. Each meeting take turns discussing what is real food in a certain part of life, work, partnership, children, church, and so on. Perhaps discuss a section of this book.

5. Practice one of the five inner steps in silence together i.e. heartfulness, understanding, forgiveness, compassion, wisdom.

6. Imagine what it would feel like; be like for each person to have a life of real food nourishing his or her soul. Where would it be? How would it be? Share the exquisite details and possibilities of real food in your lives.

7. Practice not judging others and ourselves. Make the joy support groups an example of being fully in the moment, available, and true.

# *Appendix 4.*
# *Make a Retreat*

All religions have a tradition of making a retreat. Jews celebrate the Sabbath as a day of rest and retreat. Christians go into monasteries and sacred places for a day, weekend, or longer to reflect and make a retreat. Buddhists, Hindus, Moslems, Shamans, mystics, people of all cultures through the ages have found the wisdom to make a retreat. This is taking time away from the expectations and demands of normal culture, the business of life, to be with one' self and God. Joy has fresh possibilities every time we come back to ourselves, our simple being. Making a retreat is taking the time to cultivate our inner garden, so the seeds of our natural being, our joy can grow and grow. Whether alone or with a group, in nature or a sacred place, to make a retreat is to give a great impulse to more joy in our life.

**Ten Suggestions for a Good Retreat**

1. Begin each day feeling your intention for your retreat. Let your desire for more peace, God's love, or simple peace be your first thoughts. Your intention will keep your retreat focused in the direction you want. Remembering your intention for your retreat will keep the busy world away as you look inside your spiritual path.

2. Practice being present. Catch yourself when you are speaking or thinking about things in the past or future. Be present. Here is God!

3. Simplicity. Keep a big simplicity during your retreat. Do not make your time complicated. Simplicity will always keep you close to the silence, yourself, and God's presence.

4. Do not be busy with new relationships. This is your time to be with yourself and God. The open heart naturally seeks new friends and companions. Feel your open heart and bring it directly to God. Let the love you find in your retreat be more for yourself and God inside of you. This is not a time to be making new relationships. This is a time for a new relationship with yourself.

5. Do not be concerned about what you will do after the retreat. How do I continue this experience? How do I find this peace in normal daily life? Live in the present. Receive as much as you can now. Live a good retreat. Let tomorrow come and a way will be found. Today is your day to be in retreat.

6. Distractions...the personality by its nature is busy with likes and dislikes. Don't let distractions keep you away from going deeper in your retreat. Recognize your likes and dislikes for what they are. They are not so important. The personality wants to be comfortable. This is a time for your soul. Be true to your retreat. Don't be distracted by unnecessary small talk, business, intellectual discussions, shopping, activities which do not bring you more into your retreat.

7. Time is precious. If with a group be on time. Everyone will appreciate it. If alone, be conscious of your time and how you are living your retreat.

8. Look at the choices you are making. This is the heart of the retreat. Look at the choices you are making moment to moment about where your awareness is. Where is your heart? What are you choosing to think about and do? Practice being in the retreat, as you

would wish to be in your life in general. Make choices that nourish your heart and the hearts of others.

9.  Give yourself to the retreat. In a group or alone, in nature or sacred setting, there are always distractions, too much of some things and not enough of some thing else. Our personality by its nature is busy wanting to be comfortable, in control, or exercise what "I want". A retreat is about something greater. Give yourself to the retreat. Instead of indulging your small self, who is often judgmental and critical, be with your large self. Give yourself to the retreat and you will discover much about who you really are. This is a time to soften your heart, receive your large self and that of others.

10. Be joyful! This is your retreat. There is no right or wrong retreat. This is your time, your opportunity to be more with yourself and God. May simplicity, gentleness, and truth be your guides. The retreat is your gift to yourself. Open it. Receive it. A retreat is not something to accomplish or master. A retreat is simply time with less distraction or work, a time to be more with your heart, your soul. May you find the special peace in the silence. May this peace be your best friend. Surely this friendship will grow and bring great joy for you to take home with you.

# About the Author

Bruce Davis, Ph.D. and his partner, Ruth Davis, Movement Therapist, are Americans living in Assisi, Italy. In this hilltop town of St. Francis, together they restored an ancient room from the 11<sup>th</sup> century and began **The Assisi East-West Retreat Center**. The Center, with altars to the world religions is one of the few rooms in the world inviting people of all religions to be together in peace.

The Center offers individual and group meditation retreats, yoga, and counseling. In the beauty and simple peace of Assisi, Italy the Center helps people unfold their joy and the life for their soul. Bruce and Ruth also offer retreats in various parts of Europe, Asia, and America.

Bruce is the author of **The Magical Child Within You, The Heart of Healing, Monastery Without Walls, My little Flowers,** and **Simple Peace-The Spiritual Life of St. Francis of Assisi**.

**For more information about retreats with Bruce Davis and current activities:**
**www.AssisiRetreats.org or www.sacredtravel.org**

**Assisi East-West Retreat Center**
**Santa Maria delle Rose, 2c**
**(Piazza San Rufino)**
**Assisi, 06081, Italy**

978-0-595-38868-4
0-595-38868-X

Made in the USA
Lexington, KY
09 November 2014